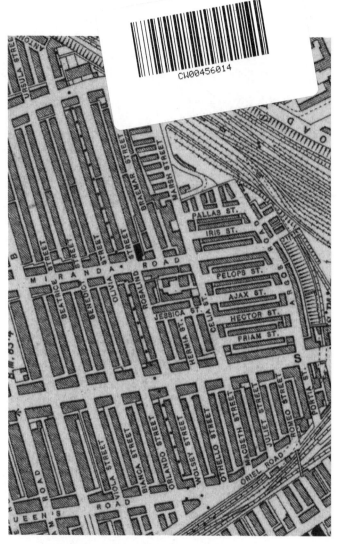

Liverpool's Shakespeare Streets, Kirkdale and Bootle, 1908
Image Courtesy of Dave Woods

TONY WAILEY

LIGHTS
BEARING WEST

Author's Biographical Note

Tony Wailey was born in Liverpool in 1947. He is the author of eight books including pocket sized novels and three collections of poetry. Originally a seaman his work concerns the cosmopolitan nature of the maritime city. He wrote *Edgy Cities* with Steve Higginson that had at its central theme the historic flows of people and ideas to and from Liverpool. His latest work concerns the context of place in the narratives of family history. In this second volume of the *Diary of the Smyth Wailey's* he still finds it amazing that his great uncle, John Brown Wailey, sailed on deck as a fully fledged Able Bodied seaman aboard a 400 ton sailing ship from San Francisco to Sydney in 1885. He was nineteen. A hundred years later Wailey was awarded a Doctorate for his work on Liverpool's Sea Going Communities and its Seaman's Union. He realises now how little he knew.

Tony Wailey

Writing on the Wall
Toxteth Library
Windsor Street, Liverpool
L8 1XF

Published by Writing on the Wall 2024
© Tony Wailey

Cover design by Daniel Turner
Layout by Daniel Turner
First page image courtesy of Dave Wood
ISBN: 978-1-916571-04-4

0151 703 0020
info@writingonthewall.org.uk
www.writingonthewall.org.uk

For George Wailey
Born Liverpool 1871
Died Bahia Blanca 1900

Acknowledgements

To Sean Garrett, Frank Kenny and Mike Morris and those many others, friends and family, who have helped me with this book.

The Quaker Graveyard in Nantucket

A brackish reach of shoal off Madaket—
The sea was still breaking violently and night
Had steamed into our North Atlantic Fleet,
When the drowned sailor clutched the drag-net. Light
Flashed from his matted head and marble feet,
He grappled at the net
With the coiled, hurdling muscles of his thighs:
The corpse was bloodless, a botch of reds and whites,
Its open, staring eyes
Were lustreless dead-lights
Or cabin-windows on a stranded hulk
Heavy with sand. We weight the body, close
Its eyes and heave it seaward whence it came,
Where the heel-headed dogfish barks its nose
On Ahab's void and forehead; and the name
Is blocked in yellow chalk.

Robert Lowell
Selected Poems, Houghton Mifflin Harcourt, 1976

LIGHTS
BEARING WEST

INTRODUCTION

Liverpool is a strange place; its identity on the Atlantic Ocean and the West coast of Europe is still defined by its river and its tides. It is a city that still moves and is moved by feelings, 'dangerously sentimental or sentimentally dangerous.' This volume two of *Diary of the Smyth Wailey's* contains that moving and often messy cultural history from the city of elsewhere. Because so many of its people have been, or are citizens of their own stories, the place constantly holds a mirror to itself about being somewhere else, even for those who have never left, it is in movement that we see the inchoate restlessness that defines its essence.

As in volume one these pages come interleaved between a family history as part of the testament of a city a cycle best described by Albert Camus in his book *The Rebel.* This story is as much about family detection as it is about rebellion. Indeed the many manifestations of a maritime culture whether expressed by individual agency or within a collective embrace in the general life of a port city is a distinction always finely tuned, and nowhere more so than Liverpool.

The first part of this book begins with an account of my great uncle John Brown Wailey, 'Bucko Johnny' around the great ports of Australia, where he spent the last two decades of his life searching for the home, he never truly found but was always alive to that possibility and died strangely at peace in the Little Sandy Desert.

The second part catalogues his father, George Alexander Wailey, my great grandfather and his final days on an Elder Dempster Steam Schooner, homebound bound from the West Coast of Africa - the classic Maggie May - before he threw himself overboard into the Celtic Sea and tried to swim across to his original birthplace of Cork.

How was he to know that of the five young sons he left behind, the eldest Bucko Johnny would go missing in that desert, Francis James would die on the last day of the third battle of Passchendaele and another George, a seafarer like himself, be murdered on the quaysides of Bahia Blanca, Argentina; or that his last two sons William Patrick and Henry would work on the docks all their lives after time at sea and in the military, unknowing but totally in keeping with that 'elsewhere' nature of Liverpool's waterfront history.

Would it be too cruel to ask, lessen the loss, cure the pain, that before those deaths, what his own absence would bestow to those sons, or to his wife and one remaining daughter, that when he took that jump in July 1887, it fell in the very same year the first Seaman's

Union was founded and which he had constantly called for in all his time at sea?

If at some strange level George thought he was going home, he left a wife Caroline (Caro) who had to bring up that young family by herself as most seafarer's wives had to do whether their husbands were alive or lost. She was still working at nearly eighty years of age in 1911 as a knocker on worker's windows to wake them, a 'Knocker Upper' in Kirkdale among the tight streets above the Canada dock, when Great Britain owned 44% of the total world's shipping fleet.

Was in all of this movement a parallel link between ships, family history and the life of port cities, that I was trying to find whilst trekking around another continent? Volume One asks that question. This one merely nods in the direction of anyone still subconsciously searching for that history inside themselves within the parameters of a great city.

When I went to sea on clean, well-lit ships a half a century after Bucko Johnny in the 1960's with plenty of food, clean bedding, and good toilet facilities, it was if the products of all those earlier struggles made on my behalf had never existed.

Did I recognize the shoulders of giants that I had stood upon? Did I hell!! except when some old salt abused us 'young fellers' with the truth of those years. '*Never forget 1911*' was George Garrett's slogan draped on sandwich boards over the shoulders of those on the picket lines in 1966. A generation before, during the Second World War, over 30,000 merchant seamen had lost their lives on the convoys across the Atlantic and Bering Sea but I was too interested in having a good time in all the ports of the Caribbean and Latin America to worry about that historical memory.

Any sense of hardship felt on my own early voyages was limited to being without air conditioning in the Western Tropics, taking salt tablets, having yellow fever injections, and using 'conny onny' instead of fresh milk. Tell that to the young soldiers struggling in the jungles of Borneo and Malaya at that time. My own time in 'The Merch' was an easy ride, full of laughs and happy occasions, even the Strikes had an air of Carnival about them, and like the young everywhere I did not know whose shoulders I had been carried upon.

With this in mind, the third part of this volume concludes with a poorly disguised autobiographical account of my own time away during the five years between 1963 and 1968. Like its predecessor in volume one its aim is to trace a social history of the city that has a deep maritime cultural thread running through it, whilst still being alive to the million personal stories that spin away yet still feed the place it is today.

To interlink any social history with personal or family life is fraught with difficulties. The writing itself brings out argumentative lines of place, memory and distance and can confound anyone attempting such an account. The link between organizations, individual action, or social agencies is entwined within such a highly contested cultural and historical space as the Liverpool waterfront.

Many years after leaving the sea I remember standing in a dockside bar with my brother-in-law when we got chatting to a couple of lads who had just walked into the old Grapes, the Cains Brewery on Grafton Street - now utterly changed into the cosmopolitan Baltic Market but then as now, still strangely in keeping with that district's maritime tradition of party and celebration.

They were talking about writers and writing. Having taken a good drink myself, I said I had just written a novel and was trying to become a writer. Our Paul nodded sagely at this but looked at me with an eagle eye, common to that part of the city; *whatever you say, say nothing.*

'Is this book about your own life's young journey?' the one with the moustache and glasses turned his head and asked.

I looked at him. With one question he had found me out. He shook his head and laughed.

'We all do it mate,' he said, 'write about something else.'

I was demolished. I still wince about it now. Forty years later; a shortened version of that novel appears here as the latter part of this volume. 'If you want to write about yourself, write about somebody else.'

By cut by contrast part of the jangle of going away was being with people who had spent a lifetime at sea; some of whom were bitter, others proud, yet others indifferent, all agreed though that time away changed you. The more time you spent there, the less real that jobs and life ashore became, the more of a mirage life became, like a shaded net curtain operated between you and reality.

'The sea is a young-man's game,' I often heard repeated

to me. 'Enjoy the ports, the stories and then get out, otherwise it fades you.'

Maybe Bucko Johnny knew what he was doing when he jumped ship around that Australian coast in the sunlight and golden dust far away from the heaving, black and congested docksides in the latter day 'famine parishes' of Liverpool's North End.

In Aboriginal lore there are specific rules for 'going back' or rather for singing your way to the place where you belong, your 'conception site,' the place where your soul is moored. Only then can you become or re-become, the ancestor; Liverpool was always in my Great Uncle's soul.

Was it true what Heraclitus said about the strange cadence of his life, that the past cracks open into a new present and all is in the process of becoming? 'Mortals and Immortals, alive in their death, dead in each other's life.' Anna Akhmatova touches upon a similar theme in her great 'Poem without a Hero' written between 1940 and 1965, 'As the future ripens in the past, so the past rots in the future.' The city was always alive to Bucko Johnny, even if he had left it a quarter of a century before.

Fade is how the mystics believed that the ideal man should walk himself home to a 'right death.' If this was the case with Bucko in the desert, in his father's case it was to swim 'home,' maddened by malarial fever and the circumstances of his last voyage. But where was home? Or my Great Uncle George's last night on the wooden boards of the quayside at Bahia Blanca; did he know the knife was coming for him there on that quayside in the December of 1900? Where was home?

Jorge Luis Borges wrote of similar deaths in many of his poems and stories of the Argentine waterfront. This echoes similar sentiments of many port city writers especially James Hanley. He who has arrived 'goes back.' But to where? And where does that leave the survivors?

At closer to 80 than 70 I'm not dead yet Deo Volante, and Liverpool is still my home, but their spirit still lives on within me and looking up, I dream every day of Ireland, the Gulf of Mexico, Australia and the Argentine and anywhere else from the wide-open skies of my own city.

Tony Wailey
3rd March 2024
Liverpool

ONE

John Brown Wailey, 1866 -1931
'Frisco, Manaus, Freo.

Some said nothing fazed the Bucko, not even when my father George took me by the scruff of the neck and sent me away from Liverpool back to Cork to join an Irish coaster, a small sailing ship that trundled from port to port around that green and cold island and carried wheat or wood and other forms of general cargo. I was fourteen.

The Old man's family were from there. They put me on the *Blarney* and ran me through the wringer when they shipped me out of *The Green Dragon* pub where my uncle had a share. Out at sea you would see the waves bursting against the headlands on the West Coast, exploding water and back on the east, the Irish Sea like a dark blue mask into which poured the Atlantic. At Galway you could feel the wind hard off the bay, a roll of cloud on the edge of the sea and the waves the colour of grim tweed the men all seemed to wear on Sundays.

It was hard going even for a galley boy I can tell you, the Bucko toiled all hours through that cold and wet summer of 1880 - a year after I had left the tender care of Saint Alexander's and started to scrape ship's boilers in the Sandon dock - one of the graving docks built for the steamship trade but then once on board this lousy sloop subjected to every spit and drag of those Irish bastards. I was Liverpool Irish. There is a big distinction.

'Ye've only come half way,' the Bosun used to sneer or worse, 'ye are only half Irish you moaning cunt.'

The tender greenish sky stood in sharp contrast to his words, a rim of light flooded up and drenched the ship, then it became ordinary daylight, the black and white landscape of water, rock and sky brought another day of thankless work. The Bucko saw it all and knew he was fucking miserable, cold, wet and miserable.

Some months later and sick of the ship's name and the ship's crew, a mean-spirited bunch if you ever saw them, I met with two American seamen in the same pub off Cobh Harbour, a bright day, spring, the water glazed and ornamented with gulls. I could see my shadow stream away from me in the blonde light of the wood wharves as we entered through the shadows of the green lacquered door.

They took me back aboard their ship, fed me and brought me back with them to the States. Down in the cabin I took a slug of their brownish liquor and stared at it, wondering what it was, this drink American sailors put down their throats.

'I don't care what *you* call me,' I said and laughed.

My blood bulged at the hot flushed limits of my face. I was happy I had said something to make grown men smile even if I had not meant to do so.

The wine was Malaga, hot, sweet, powerful, Spanish stuff. I sipped it carefully then tossed it away with dockside aplomb the way I had seen workers on the quayside do. It was sweet and hot in my belly. I smacked my lips like someone older and pulled my fist across them the way Dockers used to rub the big muscles of their forearms across their face when they had filched a drink, but I was just a kid.

'That's very good,' I said.

Something about the way I said it made them laugh again and they filled the glasses.

'He'll be three sheets to the wind,' one said.

The other one nodded at the shadow on the emptying bottle.

'This Bucko will soon be talking Spanish,' he added.

Good people. They didn't take advantage. They were a man short. I was paid wages, good money; they needed a galley lad to support that old drunken chef, a wizard for the food but a madman for the drink. It was easy compared to that Irish coaster and her tightfisted, moaning crew.

That American ship filled me up and filled me out and now I had a bit more meat on the bones, a proper middleweight's build, stocky but not too small and my teeth white and uneven and my bottom lip trying to cover the big front two so you only saw them when I jangled but I was light on my feet and could dance with anyone when they brought me wine.

But the port authorities wouldn't let me stay in New York, neither on the ship, nor in the country so I had to beat the border over to Montreal where it was easier going with the French. I liked it so much I stayed and didn't care about crossing back again. Bucko Johnny, fifteen years old and strong. I had learned something from those early trips though, that when the world closes in you have to pull your own fortune close, that the worse things get the more you have to gather yourself; you had to name your luck and wrap it around you like a warm jacket, keep it near to you from day to day as if life would always present you with more perilous journeys. I was young but I knew that. It might eventually have to die with me but there was a long way to go before that happened and chances are someone else could pick it up and carry it forward.

I loved sitting in those smoky French bars where you could look through the haze at the cold blue skies, with horse troughs outside the saloons where the farmers used to come for the markets and mix with the sailors and drink brandy and wine from up the St Lawrence. Listening to them all speaking and singing, I got my love of the Americas. It was a laugh here, rough and ready but with plenty of food and you could always earn a dollar, working kitchens, digging ditches, helping out on farms.

I was still hanging around the waterfront when they listed me in the Montreal maritime census of 1881 maybe that is where I found my love of the forests and wide spaces and just dropped in where I thought I could see something of the country. This was my life. It stayed with me throughout my time at sea, like

I say, a ship is more than just a convenience to take you from place to place. But this Bucko knew why a strange love of flowers and trees of all shapes and sizes never left him and all things Chinese and American and Australian that came with them in his time away but more importantly away from the sea and what seamen always carry inside them.

I hitched and bummed and rode the trains, flat box cars across Canada all the way, coast to coast from French Quebec in the Catholic heartlands to Vancouver and Columbia in the west. I had another crack at the border there. Eventually I beat it and took a ship from Portland down the north Pacific to San Francisco. It was where I wanted to be. Sailors were needed to go deep sea, but you could also have a bit of fun down there and the red doors of the joss houses and the gambling joints of Chinatown all served you well and became like the call of sirens with the name of *The Barbary Coast*.

Two

'Frisco was all laid out then, all wind and blue and cobble setts and hills and wharfs and you could hang around on the waterfront front nice and easy and find some quiet, solid places in the Chinese Quarter all disguised yet wild under that silent thrumming moon.

And Bucko you did some finding, up alleys, across washing lines on roofs where you could slide down into the gambling dens, lose all your money, your shirt, smoke in the opium parlors' and find different girls in each part of the place, usually up the creakers, as long as you could see the water and dive when they did at the sound of a police whistle.

The population here moved like the tides and the water was just a baby blue and surrounded you like a jewel; there were places where you could hang your washing to a bollard and listen to the soft hum of the docks long after the gold rush and the sun would dry it in places where the Clippers had berthed on jetties all around the Bay not so many years ago. The railways and the yards were finished shining new, but the fishing piers still stood out like telegraph poles along the wharves and bathed their toes in the red pools of the Bay. The whole place dipped and shimmered under the sun.

The pools were broken by rocks in places and lapped against the spars of ships riding at anchor their masts clustered together such was the weight of the traffic and almost beside them the streets spun away like silver with trash glistening in them that ran down the hills to the water's edge. The Chinese made this place their own. I liked them, they were kind and easy going and you could take time out with them in the yellow blocks of the joss houses, or folk temples and always get a meal just as long as you didn't get in the way. Bucko Johhny was just as easy as you like.

I first saw Nancy in one of those eating at houses. Maybe I was too young to know better who approached her. I still didn't know what I wanted from her but something inside me did. Her green scarf lay beside her on the chair. Her eyes were hard, but they could soften. Perhaps it was just this, to be close, to smell her scent, to look carefully at her hands, the filigree of her skin, to touch her, to eat stripped beef with her, fried and buttered in tiny bowls peeping over lettuce with spring onions and ginger. Heaven after being at sea. Maybe I just wanted to borrow money after the blowout of the last three nights. She worked at the Lucky 49 Bar.

She opened her purse, looked at me, sat back in the chair, laced her fingers under her head and spoke dreamily to the ceiling.

'You will love me tonight you fool of a sailor boy; tonight, you will love me.'

The Bucko asked, 'what am I to a woman like you?' but he didn't argue. He didn't want to get in the way.

She smiled, 'It doesn't matter. You are nobody and I might have been somebody and the path for each of us is love.'

The smell of her was pretty strong, it came mixed with another melody of poisonous variants, incense, jasmine, joss. She knew that restaurant room, that bar, the street, the whole area was hers not mine and she left that odour to impregnate every wall and every corner and every fibre of my being. I was a stranger to all this, but it didn't take me long.

I said, 'Should we take a beer outside and maybe a little walk?'

She looked at me and tightened those eyes.

'A walk around Chinatown with you; are you crazy?'

I stayed where I was.

I didn't care whether I worked or not. I hung around the harbour, drank in the bars, had a beautiful girlfriend who worked nights in the '49 er and hated the sight of water. I loved the blue mornings and the golden sunshine in the windows when she came home to Settle Street. I helped her with laundry and towels and stuff and even had to fight for her when some of the customers got too rough.

Life was great. I didn't know that all this was about to change; that they were trying to close these Chinese villages of the waterfront and that respectable white sentiment was growing. They blamed them for everything those City Fathers; the iniquity, the lawlessness, the disease, all this after what the Chinese had done to build up the place; laid their bodies down for the railroads, dug the gold fields; worked as lickspittles on the last of the clipper trades and gave up their lives when the freight companies needed more profit and sent them out as insurance on their coffin ships. Oh Yes, they were to blame all right.

The authorities even produced a map and pinned it

up on street corners showing the different districts and each one, a separate affront to the law or so they claimed. Anyone can tell you that any Chinatown is a closed place unless you know your way around.

I was lucky. I had a safe passage with Nancy whose parents were from Canton and could show me any way through the closed courtyards, the entrances and exits to every labyrinth, where one street folds into another and messages and parcels are passed through them to be handled three and four times over, just like they are in Liverpool.

What the map didn't show was what lay above or below the shop fronts; what it missed in the gambling dens two sets of creaky stairs below in the basement or the brothels one flight above and even on the attic roof where Nancy often found herself and where the better class often visited including some of those white Burghers themselves, the businessmen, the local politicians, even those from the church minus their cassocks.

It was a jumble of a place, and the Bucko loved it. You saw life in the raw and you could feel time passing through you wrapped up tight like a ball and not just hanging limp on a nail but those City fathers took care to separate the white and Chinese working girls; even then they still got the blame, that was the cruel joke, the number of Portuguese and Spanish and Italians that were down on the water as well as the Mexicans and fine Americans farm girls could be listed in their thousands but The Board of Supervisors argued that white female prostitution had only grown with the bringing of Chinese into the City.

'These women act as a magnet for others,' their pam-phlets screamed, 'a searchlight whose beam sweeps over us but leads only to the rocks.'

Tell that to the Irish in Liverpool. Talk about it in the famine parishes! If Chinese seamen were the primary patrons of white women, there they made sure they looked after them. To say that the joss houses with their tiny altars and miniature statues and offerings to the spirits were places of idolatry after their kindness had sustained me all these months, was even more of a laugh. You should come to Saint Alexanders and see the way the priests carried on after the celebrations of the May processions with the drink flowing and young altar boys serving and the smell of wine in the air.

'I know how I attract you,' Nancy said.

'And that you know about my lovers.'

'Are they like wounds to you? And the horrors that my clothes conceal? But you must try to forget about my body because I am good at heart. I am so good, and I deserve more than just your lust even though tonight you will love me sailor boy.'

The Bucko was struck dumb by her words and fought hard to keep his mouth shut. He was nineteen.

'Forgive me.' She came towards me. The tears flowed down her cheeks.

'My soul is so beautiful. It can bring you so much. It is not used and worn like my flesh, my poor body.' I wondered if she was a Catholic?

'You mustn't worry,' I said, 'You are a great woman, and your soul is as clean and shining as the stars and all this talk is an obsession; a hangover from all this anti-Chinese mumbo jumbo from the city fathers.'

I talked like that, gesturing with my hands, pleading with my voice.

'All this stuff is driving you mad, don't listen to it.'

But it was hard not to listen to her murmurings as

they went deep into the night and the voices outside grew from a tiny stream into a waterfall and cascaded down all over Chinatown.

San Frisco had been a Mission town, it held a caring Spanish soul, but the businessmen didn't want that, they didn't want anything in the way of their developments and people were fast moving across America from the East; the place was a goldmine; the Chinese were in the way.

Ship mates, old timers who had sailed the route from Sydney to Frisco showed me the Vice Map of the district they made in my time there. (1885) It used to hang above the urinals in the men's room in the Big Four restaurant on Nob Hill where we sometimes used to eat. It stayed for years afterwards. They kept it hanging long after they had razed the villages just like they had done before with the native Americans, the Ohlone, the Ramatu, the Chochenyo. You remembered how they tricked Crazy Horse before they killed him.

They remodeled the place. The Chinese quarter almost disappeared like so many others where you could have a good time; a place where you could laugh and drink and nobody cared. The map was basically part of a plan to get them out of the city. Laws followed to break the districts up in terms of space, transport, and the provision of the laundry trade. Then, they passed the Exclusion Act which virtually banned them from the inner-city boundaries. So much for the land of the free.

They raided the Lucky '49 where Nancy worked, and they pulled her in and scattered her family and a thousand others all around the Bay. She ended up in Oakland and I lost my protection. It came a couple of dreamy months later while I still worked for her house, carrying water and towels, and taking it easy down on the sunshine laden wharfs but this was the last of it.

I could have done more while I was trying to persuade her that her soul was beautiful and she was more than she thought she was, done more while telling her she was lovely and other stuff to take her mind out of the misery it was in, but I didn't. I could have done more but I didn't, couldn't give her the protection and love she had given me. Where was the Bucko when it mattered, when she really needed protection, where was I then? The sky was like a net the way it bulged with stars. He was just a sailor boy?

Three

Just as my protection ended at the Lucky '49, a gang of crimps dressed in pea jackets jumped me and enlisted me as an able-bodied seaman at the so - called China Wharf. I was to be a sailor on deck, a kingly AB, top of the game and I'd hardly done six trips my whole life but when the press gang come and Shanghai you, you're in the captain's pocket; that wasn't for the Bucko.

I'd worked with the Chinese and learned a few tricks, one of them being that you gave everything but nothing for nothing. I told the kidnappers I'd worked five years on the coastal boats and deep sea ships; I sounded like a Shellback, a Shellback at nineteen, I'd done one deep sea trip, one way!

Americans are a believing people especially those on the slow West Coast. Even those who shanghaied me took my spiel on the basis of a few voyages on the *Blarney* between Limerick and Dublin and a fishing boat called *Saginaw* around Kinsale harbour. I signed and was paid the full rate, an able-bodied man aboard the sailing ship, *The Lady Lampson*, a 400 tonner that was leaving from Frisco to Sydney next day.

Six weeks of cramming sail; a nightmare journey, learning the ropes but danger makes specialists of us all and the Bucko did his time. There was also a Chinese cook and I ate well with my few words of Cantonese around his galley door.

Australia was a golden place in the 1880's, the Pacific and Indian Ocean winds blew around every corner and the black pavement stones groaned with commerce and the sun danced on the iron tinned roofs around Sydney Harbour. That wind always brought an air of refreshment. My Da's old man, the Dada William, had run a hotel there on 238 Collin's Street in the late 'fifties before he died of drink.

George Alexander would never see him again after he left Aussie as a seventeen year old kid and came to Liverpool. I heard it was just as rough inside that place as we had it around the Roaring Forties. Drinking and laughing and shouting and full of memories of people I had not known; that was my first time down in Australia.

I was there when the Da, who'd thrown me to the wolves at fourteen on that wretched Irish hooker, threw himself overboard off the *Roquelle,* an Elder Dempster ship on the Celtic sea. Just jumped over the side and waved them all goodbye while I was shooting the coastline twelve thousand miles away.

'See you all in heaven,' someone thought they heard him say but I didn't believe that.

It was his mission to swim home to the twinkling lights of Cork harbour. Homeward bound from Dakar off the African coast, he'd shipped a bad dose of Malaria and the fever was burning him up. He felt the need to cool off; he'd tried to do it twice before as the ship made its way back to Glasgow, but it was third time lucky on that Sea where he thought he could glimpse the lights of home.

No one was going to hold him back this time. He jumped at night and in summer and for a while the water must have been a balm before he started to sink. He wouldn't have known anything about it by the time his lungs started to fill. I'm sure he must have seen those lights, but the Bucko never did. I've thought of them often and imagined him seeing them myself on many a trip back to Liverpool, but it was probably an illusion mixed up with the drink. His terrible infection and the rancid smells of the ship's cargo must have all become too much for him, (Irish Seaman's Registry of Death July 1887) because he was a hard man.

I should have said to Nancy:

'Look lady even Bucko Johnny Brown has problems of his own. He's got them too you know.'

And from under the pillow should have drawn out my father's lost rosary beads, the set he always left at home to know that with Our Lady's help, he would always return to collect them.

'Look Nancy,' I should have shown her.

'Who took them instead? I'll hold them close to you lady and then you can look into the eyes of a murderer. He would always return to collect them, but they had gone before he came home. Oh, Bucko is no angel lady so when I hold them close to you; so when I say I love you, oh beautiful Jesus, be careful. I took them away and he never came back. Forgive me; I could have done much more and even addressed those beautiful wounds that are all in your head, but I did not. I did not get justice for you or for anyone.'

Eventually we came back to New York. I hung around looking for another ship; I was now an American seaman. A wanderer of dark streets and lonely red lights the same as the seraphim of every port city. A year after the old man's death I was working the Great Lakes trade on the grain and cement boats. While I was there, I applied to the USA for Naturalization, residency and permission to work. (1888) They refused me of course. They were starting to tighten the rules there as well, but they let me stay on working as an alien seafarer.

Sometime later another good buddy of mine, Patsy Conlan was shipping out for Aussie and asked me to go with him. Young as I was, I was still too much of a ship's lawyer, a loud - mouthed complainer, a nark, always with some beef or other about conditions for those owners to want to keep me. They threatened not to ship me out but put me in jail if there was any more trouble.

I signed on with Patsy and we made the long run down again, what with one thing and another it took us almost ten weeks. Then I started thinking about my mother and the terrible crowded life she had had in those black demented court houses and dockland slums and thought of going back to Liverpool but that thought lasted about two minutes. She had enough kids to keep her company.

What she needed from me was money, time enough to go home when you were fed up with everything.

So, we shipped for Aussie and I stayed on that coast running between Melbourne Albany and Freo (Fremantle) through all the green and golden twilights of the West where the Indian and Southern oceans merge and roar and sometimes lay gentle like a sheet of pearl spread across the water. I never knew that Patsy had known my old man.

Aussie is a great place and has a great character and I stayed regular on that run for a full five years, an abundance of flowers and birds, and me sending home money regular to keep the old lady happy. We were all doing fine. You could get drunk just looking at the moon over the Southern Ocean but *malamente*, I did too much looking and a great deal of drinking too.

On one of those cold misty nights in Melbourne I had to find my way back to the Seaman's Mission all along the mish mash of twists and turns and alleys and bridges of the Yarra river that constitutes the path back to Flinders Street where the Mission sat next to the quayside.

It was at the centre of the slums that followed the goldrush of the 1860's and was a hard place to wander through even in bright sunshine; to get lost there in the dark was asking for trouble especially when drink had been taken. The Aussies love to fight, and I seemed to be fighting all along that path with anyone under the moon I chanced to meet.

The police picked me up and threw me in the jug. My name was recorded in the Melbourne Police Gazette (1893) as being drunk and disorderly and I was sent before the judge. The priest from Saint Mary's posted bail but as this was not the first time it had happened, and I thought maybe it was time for me to give these quaysides a shove before any more detention came my way; sometimes those swirling winds that came up from Antarctica got into your head and sent you crazy in these sun ridden but hard going Aussie ports.

I managed to get aboard a city boat, the *City of Liverpool* funnily enough for the jag home, I signed on for the deck and they were happy to have me there as three firemen had gone missing in Sydney and they paid better wages to the black gang. Those stokers and firemen who worked that inferno below called an engine room looked miserable and probably wished they had jumped as well. Two sailors were going to take their place. Good luck to them I thought I wouldn't work down there for a brass ha'penny; life was hard enough topside, but it was shamed brutal down in that other place.

I was going to give it a try at home, go on the dock or something but the New Unions were dragging their feet after the strike and the Port Authorities and the Shipping Federation were taking a hard line after the seamen had tried to start a national union from Liverpool but were defeated just the same as the Dockers and nobody had much of a chance or if they did they were forced back to work in lousy circumstances. (1893)

Blow them. I thought I'll give the Army a go and take the Queen's shilling like my younger brother Our Billy. He'd joined a couple of years before as a kid in 1892 and saw out his time. Billy was a small wiry little feller but like the old man, one you didn't mess with. He had a tight pockmarked face and the old man used to say he was the runt of the litter but that was before he did his first trips and signed up for the Kings regiment. Da would have kept his mouth shut had he been alive when Billy emerged from his enlistment twelve years later. He might have been small, but he was hard as nails and his hair was clipped tight to his head. He was always wary of danger which made him even more scary because you knew he had worked out the odds.

Unlike Billy the Army didn't work out for me. I'd seen too many authoritarian bastards in my time, especially those with plummy voices, leather kid gloves and hard sticks. They sent the Bucko to Ireland with Billy's old regiment the Liverpool Kings and half our battalion deserted. They must have had the same idea as me as we fanned out across the land making our own way. Seafarers didn't like bosses of any kind.

We hung about the country before they caught us and brought us back. To be honest a Scouse deserter in Ireland was not a good thing back then, they all thought we were troublemakers and insurgents even if we were only half Irish. The officers were always worried about the Liverpool waterfront and if it would rise up orange or green and spread from there to infect everywhere else in the country including back here in Ireland.

Parnell, that man of social justice, had been ditched and made to hand over to Redmond and Everton Football club were big in support of Home Rule but never mind that, they gave me three months hard labour after a trial in Dublin (1894) and it *was* three months hard; breaking stones in Kilkenny and an always cold black wind blowing down from Dundalk but the occasional whisky kept you warm or the poteen that breezed in on a cart from the country; but it was different, very different to the easy sunlight of

Australia and reminded me too much of my miserable time on the *Blarney*.

I often thought my mother, or my older sister Mary Agnes might look after me when I came back because the stones hadn't broken me, and I was fit and at 28 nearly young. They wouldn't. Too much of a hard life doesn't make anyone generous and they could see through me like a mirror especially one who had been away so long. I think they had me down in the same category as the old man because I was the eldest son.

Mary Agnes, my older and best sister, would not have it. The heat of the summers always spilled over her, the longest days, those of hunger or the belt seemed to bewitch her, that same force that gives form to the rebellious flesh and melded the bones of her face into a strange beauty also made her tough. She wanted more freedom not less.

'I've done enough of my looking after, Johnny,' she'd say. And named in order both the first and second names of my four younger brothers and what she had to do to help our poor Ma in seeing to their wellbeing. She enunciated their names again slowly, like reciting the catechism, one by one of those who had followed me out of our mother's tired womb.

She shook her head. 'No more of that for me Bucko,' she said.

She also had to face down the pain of a drunken first husband who beat her for being beautiful, and the pain that was also bestowed upon her by the rumours that she had contributed to his death, had even had a hand in killing him. This hurt her even more, that she had lain in wait and laid him low; with everyone in the tenements saying that they knew who the real killer was, or worse, the instigator and they looked at her with angry delusional eyes.

They said James Robinson her husband must have had some reason to beat her. They would then cackle, the owld Biddies and Mary Ellen's in their black shawls on their way to market but Mary Agnes would always hold her head high and give back as good as she got.

'Maybe she couldn't give him what he wanted,' they said.

'Maybe youse have never had it,' Mary Agnes would evenly reply.

'Oh, blessed Jesus' they said; 'Isn't it strange that she's the recent widow of a drunken seaman and how she manages to go out dancing.'

And they said, 'Is it so strange that she just happens to fall in to being the fiancé' of a shipping clerk, with that poor man not yet cold in his grave.'

That poor man; James Robinson, a nightmare more like. The Bucko would have killed him himself if it wasn't the drink. Some said that there was more than just a slip when he staggered home drunk up Falstaff Street but that was just tittle tattle. He came home as usual, home in a stupor, morning or night, this time in the dawn from a night's work on the twilight gang and had his head smashed like an eggshell on a doorstep before ten o'clock one shining morning. He never made it back to Othello Street.

He was a seaman like all of us and a Docker when he could be bothered on one of the thousands of ships that visited the port. He'd gotten used to the drink and it was the drink that killed him. In Liverpool when we were young being drunk   was all around us, from morning to night, more in this city than anywhere else on these islands. It only depended on you having the money. Around the North end docks there was a pub for every hundred people. Across England one would do for two thousand. They said it was the wind from Ireland that made us thirsty and blew us to New York but they never knew the hunger.

It was true Mary Agnes liked to go out and dance and that's where she met her 'better class of person.' Groups of young shipping clerks would often go out and search for 'Irish' girls to accompany them to parties, often in the rooms above the kegs, gin bottles and rum barrels of the 'slum pubs' on the dock road. Little wonder she wanted away from all that.

Frank Clegg was one of the thousands that served the waterfront from the City's offices. Besides the Dockers there were many other categories of workers like himself, recording, invoicing, tabulating and accounting. In numbers there was probably more of them or not far short of those who worked on the quaysides. They had security and a small but steady income that guaranteed a more regular way of living, but they were not much better off than us and they also had to keep up appearances; genteel poor, they wore patched black suits and it could not disguise the considerable poverty that they had to endure in contrast to our families who lived day to day and penny by penny but enjoyed all the rough comforts of the poor.

Mary Agnes was a good sister but her going off and getting married interrupted my plans that she was to stay home and look after me. We would get a house, and I could go away and come back again to see them all with money in my pocket. I didn't know then about her plans. Or what was to happen.

Down here on the river every piece of space was spoken for; the waterfront squeezed repair yards, ropemakers, soap and dye works and rolled them into one roaring smoky mass. Between them lay over two thousand closed Courts, thirty families in two ramshackle buildings, just like ours from South to North along the river, where the overhead railway ran down through every brown piece of line to link the docks. Nearly ninety thousand lived here, fought, lived and died in these slums. We could have been in our own gold rush. Little wonder Mary Agnes wanted space. It made China-town in 'Frisco look like a well laid out suburb. Our Mary didn't want any more of that, nor the insults and the sad rattle of the crowded, chiding poor, no matter what she said in return.

She was a happy woman when she became engaged then married Frank the only question was if he would let her continue to go out dancing because she liked that and a drink of wine and a Hooley back home on the dark landings where many a poor soul was conceived between floors and born on the wrong side of the blanket.

'Who does she think she is?' asked the old ones looking in on the dancing with their oil lamps and their night buckets but Mary Agnes was marrying away from them and that for her was all that mattered. They could say what they liked; call her what they wanted but she was going to be gone from them now; the gone woman.

The Bucko joined in their celebrations but one sleepy afternoon in Kirkdale with just the steady hum of trams and horses and the workings of the docks below in the sunshine and a couple of somnolent drinks inside me, somebody said the Cunard were taking on seamen. Six months at home was enough for anyone so I beat it across to Bank Hall and raced down to the Huskisson dock and signed for that shipping Company and an hour later took the last slot on the liner, The *Lucania* as a sailor on the deck; I was going back to sea.

THE LUCANIA

The Bucko joined this Cunard Liner as an able-bodied seaman after deserting from a brief spell in the army and following a military trial in Dublin. The Lucania was a big ship plying between Liverpool and New York. John Brown Wailey joined her and started working on the deck. The year before his death George Wailey Bucko's younger brother would work aboard her as a stoker.

I stayed on the *Lukey* for nearly two years and enjoyed it, those quick runs back between Liverpool and New York suited me, but as always the urge to jump or back out came along and if there was a chance of work on one of those Brooklyn piers or a shift on the barges, on the Jersey, the Hudson, or the East rivers I'd take it, anyone would, the money was that good.

The whole of New York was one great watery basin, over 350 miles of it from Staten Island to the New Jersey shoreline; no wonder the Port Authority was the great leading public institution of the City; boss of the rivers that encircled it and master of the island boroughs, all else fell in silent homage before its power.

The Bucko thought he'd lie low here for a bit to clear the head of soldiering. They still wanted to claim me those bastards in the English Army; even after my trial they were still on my tail. The Cunard couldn't have cared less but if you're from Liverpool both of them, the White Star shipping company or the Military authorities all leave a mark on you. They left it on Bucko Johnny.

My brother George, the next after me of our four brothers took my place on the ship but that wasn't until he had also joined and run away from the Army.

His trial was held in Lancaster (1896) two years after mine, but he wasn't there. In absentia, he was on the run again. He went onto the docks under a different name and back to sea, mainly shipping out of Newark or Hoboken.

Five years after my court martial (in 1899,) I used to meet him over on New York's West Side and we'd go for a drink around Twelve Points and Chelsea. We'd talk about our home in Kirkdale and laugh and recall what sort of place it was. I wasn't worried, I always knew I could get a quick berth off that front if I needed it. In Liverpool we used to call it a Pier Head Jump. If anything was happening back home, I knew I could always get back in time. A jump like that meant you could be in your house for tea or sucking an orange on your way to Argentina.

George was back and forth across the Atlantic like a homing pigeon. There were thousands of us like that funneling their way this way and that across its gray and blue waters. New York was that sort of place, the same enticing draw as the Aussie ports or for foreign seamen the Liverpool waterfront, they were places of comers and goers with bright lights and plenty of bars for company. You think you'll stay for a couple of trips and next thing you know years have gone by.

In New York the streets were full of Horses, men, guy ropes, enormous stones, worms, heaps of orange peel and rubbish stacked as high as the nearby Third Street hospital. What an embarrassment for the port authorities, there is nothing down here but a stinking mess, few bandages, no cures, no nurses, no drugs, no ambulances, no beds, no doctors, no laboratory, no plasma, no syringes, not enough operating rooms but thousands of us seamen and refugees from all over the world. Not everyone is hurt, not everyone is sick, but everybody wants to get by; and everybody needs a drink. The Bucko loved it.

Then George would suggest we have a couple more, he'd always want another one, and laugh and then say about the likenesses to our own City, 'but its home,' he'd say and after a shot or two it really would seem warm back there; Mary Agnes would look after me or so I thought and Ma too if she was not too busy with the younger ones.

My brother George was the second son of our mother Caroline Brown and named after his father George Alexander Wailey and born into the black, court tenement off the dock road in the April of 1871. He was christened at Holy Cross, in the June of that year and like me he went first to the Cork Shipping Company and was put on the Irish Coaster the *Gavin*.

He went deep sea a couple of years later when he joined the *Oxenholme* as a Trimmer, carrying coals to the stokehold and the firemen. She was an emigrant ship that ran between Liverpool and Montreal. George was always at home and then always away and in those three years between 1892-5 he worked both as seaman and a longshoreman in New York. After his trial George used to say that he knew more about the Americas than anyone.

'And don't let them tell you that Liverpool dockers don't know anything of that great poem across the water,' he used to say.

He said he knew New York better than he did the famine parishes of his own city and liked it better as well, free from the tribulations of the military. He liked the fashion and the good money. He always wore his trousers short, half-mast and used to affect a bleacher cap. We used to laugh at his white socks. They got him into many a scrap, but he looked a picture, even at his wedding I think they were a lemon off white and highlighted the straps on his highly polished shoes.

After 1897 until the sunshine years at the end of the century he is listed as a seaman, dodging between different companies and even going on the Norwegian Pool when the search parties got too hot back home. They generally reckoned that if you beat the military tentacles for a year or more they left you alone. George wouldn't work in a factory or on the land where you were static and could be picked off sweating under the sun and presenting a sitting target. You could move around easily in the ports or at sea. They couldn't come for you so easy there.

He worked hard aboard his first big Cunard Ship the *Carpathia* 1898 as a Trimmer, hurrying coal to the furnaces. And in 1899 – 1900 he's aboard my old ship the *Lukey,* where he does five trips to New York and gets promoted to Fireman; but he does not join the ship for one trip in October 1899 (Shipping Records) in order to marry his long-time girlfriend Mary Jane Ross.

Red haired Mary- Jane; she wore a white ribbon in it at their wedding.

'Same colour as your socks George,' someone said and everybody laughed.

'Aw fuck off,' George said but he laughed as well.

There were four weddings out of our house in that year between 1899 – 1900 when three of my brothers took wives, George and Mary Jane, Francis James and Rose Smith and our youngest Henry and Catherine Naylor. Apart from the last one they were all conducted on the waterfront as was Billy's with Nelly Flanagan when he came out of the army in 1903. The Bucko attended every one of them except Henry's who got married in Saint Alphonse's a protestant church up by St Domingo's Pit two miles from the water, we wouldn't go up there.

I didn't know then that George was clearing his book just like I had to do many years later. If I had known at the time, it would have saved me a lot of anguish, thinking it was me who had persuaded him to leave the big ships and go back on the Cargo. He'd been seeing Mary Jane for some time even if we didn't know if her son was his.

'She has a little feller William,' he says and just grins at us.

The kid was six when they got married but it didn't matter to George. They stood in Saint Anthony's in the Indian summer of October 1899 and then had a party. After two weeks he tries to re-join his ship again, but his place was taken. He'd left too quickly and without enough notice but that was our George for you. There's a picture of him and Mary Jane; she wears a white suit and has a ribbon that streams from her shining hair and there's him with his socks showing and his thick muscular frame and he's laughing too into the camera.

They all lived down on the front in Kirkdale, on Major Street, Buckingham Place, and Georges Terrace even on Sterling Street where our Ma was now decamped. Maybe it was me talking to him about going back on the cargo when he suddenly decides not to wait for another good job with Cunard but joins the *Leuctra* a Jones Boat in the November of that year.

The *Leuctra* is a small and newly built and weighs only 3000 tons. Why didn't I figure it out? In some ways the Bucko is slow to catch on. The trip is from Liverpool to Buenos Aires and then down to Bahia Blanca. No one knows him there but there are British agents all over the eastern ports of the States, especially New York. Maybe I just didn't figure what he'd done on that big Shipping Company, maybe it was nothing and he just couldn't bear to stand still.

The crew go ashore in Bahia for a night. It's just after Christmas down there but the weather is hot, and they need a drink. Something must have happened in the bars, some insults slung, some woman opportuned on the dance floor because on their return to the ship a mass brawl breaks out on the quayside (Mole' C, Quay C) and George is stabbed in the heart by one of the millions of Spanish or Italian Workers in an argument over women, over drink, over anything; probably women, given the great difference in numbers between males and females among the millions of immigrants pouring onto the Argentine then.

The official record our Ma received read, 'stabbed through the heart, death instantaneous' on the night of the 28th December, at Bahia Blanca, Our Lady of Buenos Aires.

'He left those big ships to get properly away and now he's gone for good.' Mary Jane sobbed.

She did not know the reason either but there must have been one. Later she said.

'It was just a brawl, just a stupid quayside brawl, but you know George, he had to be involved in everything?'

I could have asked if women had sparked it, or had he been robbing off the Cunard, but I didn't. She would not have known anyway, but the fact is less than 18 months into our poor George's married life, Mary Jane is a widow with an eight-year-old boy.

I was in New York when I heard about the murder. They recorded his death while I was staying in Brooklyn, and it nearly killed me. They buried him in Bahia and noted it in the 'Deaths of Seamen Registrar' of that year. The *Leuctra* sailed back to Hull in January 1901 with a cargo of Linseed Oil.

George was best man at Mary Agnes's second wedding in the Spring of 1900, when she had the first dance with Frank Clegg. By the time the national Census was taken in April 1901, Mary Jane records only herself and the boy, and both are thrown out by her father to live with her sister's family, the Jones's, in another packed court tenement on Great Homer Street on the corner by the old Fever Sheds, the same sheds that housed the human cattle off the Irish Ferry who tottered down the planks like a series of wooden skeleton onto the quaysides north of the Clarence dock. The coffin boxes they used to call them.

George was like me and a thousand others from where we come from who shifted in and out of jobs between the sea and the port. We earned our living and lived our lives among the many bits and pieces offered there, the bigger the docks the better. Besides the quaysides and the ships, themselves there were riggers, humpers, glampers, splicers and gig and tugboat men. It was always likely that, this way of life and our way of thinking, ducking and diving, that carried us well beyond the boundaries of any taste of salt or colour of bricks.

We thought of ourselves as *free men* even if those words did not always meet the reality of tyranny, authority and separation that governed our lives aboard ship. We emigrated for work, as well as jumping for the change of scene, sometimes for years at a time, to places like New York, Virginia, and the Carolina's, ports that studded the East coast of America and when the United States started to close up, the next place of escape was on the Argentine where British rails, coal and steel had built the country and linked the cattle stations to the ports; the ports that carried away my poor brother.

The Bucko wept as the immigration from Spain, Southern Italy and the Eastern Mediterranean began to fill the huge spaces of the cities and the pampas. Who was he to disagree? They all met at the quayside, a violent melting pot in those dangerous places frequented by gauchos, dockers, criminals and seamen where they drank hard and fought hard at the Pulperias and taverns that dotted the waterfront like dark sentries, sawdust at their feet and wine in the air, women made it more dangerous.

There was always the threat of the sudden eruption of violence. Maybe George had started that fight or just got caught up in its aftermath. For our poor Georgie, neither the Army desertion nor jail put an end to his career as a seaman, a docker or a recently married man but he paid a heavy price for that night ashore in the Christmas of 1900.

Maybe it was here, full of sadness at his death that the Bucko gained solace at the sight of flowers. I found a sense of repose in the not too long ago completed north side of Central Park, especially the quiet part that overlooks the reaches of the East River. I must admit, I started there but wandered bit by bit, up and down the thousand streets Manhattan has to offer; his death was a blow to me, and I'd take a drink wherever I could.

Afterwards, the buildings of the big city began to draw in and enclose me. I tried each of the eleven states that constitute the American Mid-West. I had a buddy who was part Sioux and he told me to visit the Lakota who lived across the Michigan peninsula and over to that other State where the villages existed in a thin red line all the way through the great Sandhills that constitute the northern part of Nebraska and led up to the Dakotas.

'They form a particular bridge of American life,' he told me.

'If you want to find a way through pain, go and visit them. Think of us as the early nomads and what we've had to go through to please the bankers, the landowners, and the planters to see how entrapment damages your health. Visit our reservations on Pine Ridge, it'll help you understand.'

Maybe they remembered Bucko was part of my name; and the way I could talk of the murder of Crazy Horse in that shuttered compound of Fort Robinson or the way they closed down the Chinese villages in San Francisco and added *Despedida* to my appellation when I was working the Amazon.

Stone Cloud called me out to tell me to visit those barren pits that are like beads of rain through an empty mist where there had once been such plenty in body, mind and soul.

'Look at our history from the wheat fields of the prairie to the Swede towns that are mushrooming all over the Mid-West,' he said with a sad shake of his head.

I went in such a spirit to rid myself of all the bad thoughts and why George was not still with us and what still might still lie open before me. I visited the places he told me across the slow dull towns of Wisconsin and the bored swollen ones of Ohio and the separate districts and regions and the whole of Catholic Minnesota. I felt so lonely with his death that I wanted to ride through every state of America just to put some space between me and his murder and to try and rid from my mind the sad act that became his end.

Four

It might have been there in the state of Nebraska, when the brilliant sun struck the Bucko like the chain of life itself and the idea fell like a golden link in a shower across the plains; swirled around into the light the way it did in Aussie; simply the best way to help the Ma and all the kids at home, not by sending more money and getting out from under her feet but just the opposite, stick and twist. The Chinese had taught me that. I would marry Mary Jane. So simple in the way it brought so many things together, the Bucko thought himself a genius and showed what you can do as you get older. Instead of finding a woman to relieve him of such sadness at his brother's death he would return home and conjoin with his widow, his squaw, his Mary Jane.

That is what the brothers of the early Americans had done; I would follow the lead of Crazy Horse. It strengthened as time passed and I rode the land, on the pad, by hoof and by boxcar all across those open spaces that constitute the middle heart of North America.

The thought of all the pain at my brother's murder and the manner of its coming receded before me like the hills and instead another ache rose inside me but this one carried the swell of love. We have our best moments when we're away. It is why Liverpool is an elsewhere city, always out there somewhere on the horizon under blazing sunshine or twinkling stars. If my mission was to celebrate George what better way than to help us both, me and his widow than to come together in his memory. Little William would not even have to change his name. It delighted me. Our tears are never for the dead but what they leave behind.

Waiting for the sound of the train in the middle of the fields, in our Sunday rags, small town Mid-West, conversing, sharing the contents of our pockets in the sunshine, without the worry of embarkation without fare, the stress of running alongside the cars, the hiding behind the rust red water tower, iron cross ties, brown handled switches on shining tracks, angry guards, hoping with blissful quiet certainty that no absurd train will come in all this yellow sunshine to break the sweetness of the waiting moment, scarce a penny between us, in this way tears were chased in the knowledge of sweet purpose.

The bums would help me in better ways than money. Thinking back on it, it was a single moment of kindness that brought these thoughts to their beautiful realization. That afternoon in Nebraska a well-dressed woman gave me a silver dollar. On those boxcars and with those bums it was a fortune. All around those northern and Mid-Western towns, I shared it out and made good friends. They concurred with my plans; I would only do what the Old School did, bunk in with your dead brother's squaw; do the right thing, marry Mary-Jane and keep the family name and my mother's sanity. Red haired, black eyed Mary Jane with her slight dancers frame and wild bleak humour, a drinker and a twister who loved to throw her head back and emit sheets of laughter out of that thin body, swaying as if she was playing a musical instrument with all she could shout and sing with the best of them at any party. The bums said they would love her; my turn now?

By the time I crossed those States every engineer, every conductor, even the Bulls and Pinkerton men knew my plan, from Milwaukee down to Chicago and back up to Saint Paul. It took me some time to return to Liverpool, but I did it after riding through the wheat country to catch a berth out of Duluth on the great lakes, a grain boat that came through the canals and Saint Lawrence River and then with scarcely a hitch, across the wide Atlantic on a Cunard boat from Pier 54, off Twelfth Street Manhattan.

The ship would drop me off on my doorstep at the Huskisson dock. Our district was also called Sandhills and where we lived in Kirkdale was right in the heart of the docks within the maze of adjacent streets that lay above the Huskisson and Canada basins. If it was all the same to old George our father trying to swim back to where he had come from and drowned for his trouble, it must have been the same for our George, getting involved in that stupid fight on the quayside of Bahia, Argentina but it wasn't the same for the Bucko. I was full of life and I wanted to get back to Liverpool as soon as possible to get married.

I loved Mary Jane despite all my tears for George. From the moment I caught sight of those liquid black eyes and her love of wine and dancing, I knew it, even at their wedding reception held in the Rotunda Social Club on Scotland Road. I wanted to get back for her; I'd done enough thinking; all I could worry about now was how my return would affect the situation.

They used to say on the old clippers, the one that took me from 'Frisco to Fremantle, and then around the wool and meat wharfs of Melbourne that if in a dream a man commits adultery with another man's wife, the victimized and cuckolded husband has the right to inflict the worst punishments on that other man, by fire, by water, by iron, anything. The adulteress for her part should be forgiven to continue in her ways. That was the way I looked at things. It is a strange religion that gives no account to directions south of the belly.

Before I took the jump back to Liverpool, I saw the *Lucania* at her pier, a jewel amidst the rubble of the waterfront. Poking out from behind her after end were the sleek portside offices of the Cunard Shipping Company with its green glass windows and the company moniker stamped proudly across them in gold. I badly wanted to return, but I couldn't do it, not on that ship, thinking of the time both myself and George had sweated int her subterranean stokeholds. I could see his stocky frame shoveling hard alongside me even if time and the deck had separated us. I stepped aside from the polished wood and stone of that great building into the lilac afterglow of the harbour where water and sky joined together, and the lighthouse lay green on the point and the air smelled like roses instead of the usual molasses and tar and waited instead for the old *Mauretania*.

The *Maurie* was scrapped some years later in 1908 but the memory of George who worked the *Lukey*, his last big ship was just too much for me. There were firemen aboard who knew both of us and the jangle would have been too painful; of past trips and ships and other seamen we knew. I could afford to wait a day or two for the runs were thick and fast between that Queen of American ports and the Liverpool river.

I knew when I got home, I was going to stay. Our Billy, the silent hard case was just coming back from the Army and would have the call of a brother on the dock. He was the third of us five and was waved onto the Canada quays by his future father-in-law Thomas Flanagan who delayed his retirement to get him a place down there. Thomas was a long timer at the Canada.

After leaving the sea The Flan as they used to call him worked at the docks for nearly twenty-five years. He was about the same age as my old man but had the sense to come ashore when he was in his 'forties. Another child of the Irish famine, he remained a steady worker throughout his years on the river. It was only later we found he also had family in New York but we didn't know anything about them except his American lover shared the same name as the woman I wanted to marry, Mary Jane.

'It's Nelly's dowry,' Thomas Flanagan spoke for his daughter.

Billy, her husband, was born eight years after me in 1874; he was eight when I was sixteen and so I only remembered him as a child. There was a small universe between us. I hardly knew him but as he grew older he was a short sea seaman; an army man and a docker just the same as us all, but I didn't know if George's death affected him the same as it did the Bucko. That's the thing with different ages between children, you never really catch up. It will be the same with the kids today.

Me and Billy worked well enough together and often tramped home side by side through the quiet sunlit streets of summer. I liked old Thomas as well and he liked me. And similar to my old man, he used to talk about the wool wharfs of Brisbane and Sydney and Melbourne in the 1860's; the same way as George Alexander did in his own day of sailing before the mast. Billy only got married when he was near thirty , so he wasn't a young man and had a pension from the Army. He did those military years straight on the bounce before coming back home . We drank in the Banjo pub just over the cobbles from Wolsey, Othello and Orlando Streets where all our family lived and took many a drink and held many a night there. I stayed at home on the docks and lived between them all.

Nelly Flanagan worked with Mary Jane on the ship's

laundries. She knew of my plans and provided any glue of an excuse that could help the Bucko achieve them. She took me with her whenever there were any messages needed delivering between our houses. There were always women in ours considering my Ma had so many boys. Mary Jane might have changed her name back to Ross when she was widowed but she wanted to keep George's surname for her son, maybe in memory of that fateful night. Nelly made sure that Mary Jane could meet me at every possible opportunity.

She'd wave her huge hands and laugh at her own antics whenever she included me. What you noticed about Nelly was the size of those plates, they were huge and red and shiny from constantly being in water and possessed knuckles the size of cherry tomatoes, fists any prize fighter would have been proud of but she was also a great persuader without ever resorting to force; a big laughing, stout woman, very steady and honest and just as nobody on the dock road would mess with her husband; nobody messed with Nelly least of all himself. Her strong features masked the tragedy of having no child of her own, but it did not echo in her kind manner.

When everyone knew our George was foolhardy and always up to some trick or other, Billy became notorious for caution. His nickname on the dock was 'watch yer step,' always backing away from anything that looked suspicious. The docks were notorious for accidents. Perhaps being under fire so many times in his life Billy knew how easily a life could be changed or snuffed out by a second's inattention.

'There are place you are never supposed to be,' he would say, and no-one knew whether he meant Africa, Argentina or the timber wharf at the end of our street.

I stayed on the docks with Billy and Nelly for a couple of years and just made short coastal trips now and then to keep my hand in. I lived with them when they were still trying so desperately for children but to give them space, I crossed over from Othello to Wolsey Street and lodged with Francis James and his wife Rose.

All twenty-six streets around our teeming district were named after one of Shakespeare's characters hence their name as 'the Shakey's.' They were well named considering the number of pubs we had around us bred restless, dramatic lives and provided a better home for many than those darkened grim Courts with thirty families around a lightless square. This was all we knew when we were growing up and where my brothers were brought blinking into the candlelit gloom. These new streets were good ones for us, crowded as they were, with the river below and the Stanley Road above us running through the city on its way out to Bootle, Seaforth and Waterloo and followed the same direction downstream. They were happy houses.

Francis James- had two small kids by this time, Edward James and Georgina. Francis was a house painter and his broad chest reflected this fact even if, in contrast to Nelly, his hands were tiny. He was an easygoing tall man, the tallest of us boys and generally wore a broad smile. Because he was easygoing, they welcomed me; confident in the knowledge that he and his wife Rose, would have many more children and I could move on then. When things became more relaxed at Billy's, Nelly took me back again where they had more space, but she still could not conceive and if that was a tragedy it still did not stop her feeling sorry for me. Maybe she felt she was giving back this way, getting me in tight with Mary Jane and the family and not losing me to the absences of going away.

Nelly was born in the same year as my youngest brother Henry and besides her hands she was heavy jowled and some said lumpy, but she had the light of an Easter candle shining in her eyes; two years older than Mary Jane she knew how to handle her. She also had a wild sister; their Katie who bore just the same imprint as Mary Jane and so Nelly knew first- hand what form parties and drink could take in the manner of mad dancing and accompanying fiery temper.

They were always in each other's company. Mary Jane liked nothing better than to go out and fling herself about and all Nelly wanted to do was stay home, say the rosary and look after children. Nelly was desperate for children. Each month was a separate death. I was a welcome distraction.

Nelly had lived and worked all along the spine of the waterfront districts north of the Landing Stage from Vauxhall through to Bootle; from Scotland Road to Stanley Road and then to Marsh Lane, legendary for its Western Ocean stokers that served the big ships at the Alexander, Hornby and Langton Docks. The way children were shelled out like peas from spit and saw-dust pubs to every seagoing family along that stretch of river except hers brought long days of sadness, but I don't know if Billy was that bothered even if his seed didn't take. He'd seen too much stuff in Africa. He worked every shift going. Even with his medal and a pension from the army, Nelly understood the need for credit and the pawnshop.

Nelly was as good as her word. She knew I was soft on Mary Jane and tried to help me in all sorts of ways. She'd take me around with her to babysit little William. Maybe later things might start to happen; they knew each other because their families had grown up on the same streets of Wolsey and Othello and Orlando together and when they started to work, there was a history between them and even though there was two years difference, that soon changed when they danced the mad hours the laundries demanded when the big ships came alongside.

Mary Jane would say, 'Come and help me with the little one,' and Nelly would put down what she was doing and tell me. She knew it would give me a chance to visit before she went out and when she came home. Mary Jane went out a lot and would often come back with her long red hair tumbling over her shoulder when she had been swung around at the dance or on the wine. Work was always a bridge between them.

Nelly was steady, Mary Jane was feisty. She drank and she liked it. Her mother drank wine, and she liked it too but her old man hardly took a drink and his only pastime lay in his scowl. Johnny Sour his mates called him. The Bucko and Mary Jane had a couple of little moments together on walks to the Sandhill's. We went sometimes to the markets, but it wasn't enough for her to go along with any of my big plans.

If you lived anywhere near the river, then you lived near a market. They were spread up and down like mushrooms along the Mersey. Mary Jane used to go with her mother but then sometimes she would come with me; 'for the air,' she'd say.

We'd walk down Scotland Road to St Martin's or Paddy's as everyone used to call it ,where everyone did their shopping and walk between pushcarts on the curb and the open stalls in the tenements and every one of the stall holders would be competing with the same oranges and apples and tangerines and bananas coming in regularly on the Fyffe's boats, a ha 'penny a pound, tuppence a pound, two for a penny, two pound for three pence, they'd shout. The Traders wrote their prices on paper bags and hung them like brown flags on wooden slats behind each fruit crate or vegetable box but even that wasn't enough, they'd call out their wares with little phrases and scatter them with innuendo and other jokes.

'Look missus I got the best.' He'd hold up two oranges.

'Feel these sweet juicy things.' Everyone would laugh,

'Smell these apples lady, fresh from Canada you won't get a bigger wind to blow over them.' More laughter.

They talked, they cajoled and the women out shopping shouted back. You couldn't feel bad in all this urgent, rushing mass so close to the water and the windward life that came with it. Where did that roll of carpet come from? How did such a box of shoes appear next to a heap of carrots ? What was that woman doing wearing so many cardigans? If someone shouted out his prices were too high, you could bet your life one of them would answer back with lines like.

'Everyone plays on me, Lady.'

'Is that you or your Piano?' More guffawing and the men joining in or looking on with knowing smiles where everyone who worked down there bore the halter of a nickname.

The one they called the Balloon; always sighing 'Don't let me down girls.'

There was chatter and the smell of horses and kids darting from side to side and the overhead railway roaring over its stanchions and people inside looking down and people in the market looking up at the wooden box cars rattling above them and dockers coming away from ships and others down on their luck shambling along looking for breakfast or someone to buy them a cup of tea. Others sat at the café's and read their morning papers and smoked and laughed and joked.

The old families had the real quality stores where you walked in and bought your chickens still in their feathers or your fresh fish or pork chops or milk or butter or cheese that had come in from the country that they wrapped in special paper or dug pickled onions out of huge jars with glinting metal prongs. There were bargains to be had all over Paddy's market. The Bucko loved it.

Mary Jane said, 'George used to bring me here.' I nodded unhappily.

We were all children of the markets like we were of the river, but these trips weren't getting me very far despite all of Nelly's promptings.

We never really did do it me and Mary- Jane, well only a couple of times, after George was well buried, but it was more out of sympathy, kindness, a good drink of whisky and a little shared warmth on her part rather than to see me as anything else; but certainly not as a husband . George was dead. She wasn't being unfaithful.

I loved her – all my travelling had shown me that, I'd even take on her little kid Billy, the way our George did. She might have been red headed and fiery and a dancer to boot but she wanted more from life, just like Mary Agness who married Frank Clegg to get out of the Courts but found after marriage that he was boring, and she later became fat and callous. It didn't matter to Mary Jane, she wanted something beyond the comings and goings of the sea and I did not fit the picture.

Her old man was the manager of a dock warehouse. When Mary Jane married our George in October 1899. He was not only down below on the *Lucania* as part of the black gang. *But too far* down below in the pecking order according to her old man

'Still a trimmer at 28,' he'd splutter, 'a coal drag, a bum.'

George's murder seemed only to convince him of a seaman's unsteady ways, partially induced by those events and stories about those who went away all around him with their talk of Calcutta and Antofagasta and Melbourne as indeed the everyday talk of the Americas within our family. I was closest in line to his bad humour. After George's death, Mary Jane didn't stay long in that house where they lived on Celia Street, she wasn't allowed to.

The Scowler threw her out, because of her waltzing abroad to brightly lit places on the Dock Road where music and drink could be found aplenty; 'Knocking Shops' he called them. It didn't matter to him whether she was Catholic or Protestant, or had a young son, he just wanted her out of his house and whoever was with her. Those streets could be cruel.

She constantly argued, the mother screamed and pleaded for her but the Da was unforgiving, implacable. He didn't want any more of her. He thought he had got rid of her when she married our George. Imagine what he felt like when she started walking out with me. Even those who knew him well recalled his bad temper.

'We've seen enough of that lot,' he used to say about our family.

After some months she went to live on Great Homer Street with her sister's family, her husband and the kids, the Jones's. Davy Jones was another easy going docker and he and his family lived in number 5, 12 Court. There was not much space there but when I went around with Nelly to see Mary Jane, they always made us welcome...

I knew that she had been seeing another man, a pork butcher from the southern midlands who had set up shop on Burlington Street. Maybe she just didn't want to marry another seaman, no matter how much she liked me and how well we got on together. There was no contest between the Bucko and that Butcher.

Mary Jane knew what she was getting with him. She had another two kids before five years was up but knew in her heart, she was secure, something she never was with our George no matter how much of a laugh they had together when he was home. Maybe she could see what my mother Caroline had to endure along with other seamen's families with their long absences and ashore, the constant demands of food, drink and love.

When she married G F Newbold from Leicestershire who had come to make his money in the city, it was like a death knell to the Bucko, a May Day signal, a semaphore in strong code. She didn't want anything more to do with me, especially someone ten years older and maybe too set in his ways. Much as she liked the dancing and the drinking, she wanted someone who was there all the time and like Mary Agnes, wanted to feel secure.

I remember her hands uselessly shredding the paper serviette at a pub we used to drink at just by the market, *The White Horse*.

'This is the last time Johnny,' she said in a quiet voice.

My hands felt heavy, worn. I wanted to caress hers, place them on top of the bar and hold them there.

'The last time,' I repeated her words.

Both of us knew we didn't want to lie. She looked at me with genuine anguish. We both knew what emotion gets stirred up with drink and how little we had genuinely shared together despite my big plans. The memories of our poor Georgie seemed to echo in our shared sadness, and we couldn't get away from it.

'I need a home not a roof Johnno,' she said.

The day she married she said to Nelly.

'Those wild days are behind me girl.' It made me feel sad.

She lived in that part of the city where the population reached 140,000 per square mile, a higher density than anywhere else in the world. She was only 25 when informed of Georges murder but for her old man that was time enough to get rid of her and any more of her shenanigans. She didn't need me, and it was only a matter of time before she met the Butcher, or someone like him. He loved that lovely red hair like I had done and like my sister Mary Agness, Mary Jane Ross was sick of the courts and the tenements, and the lives of the poor piled up like blackened bricks and laid on top of one another.

I often wondered if she thought of what went through George's mind in that moment before his death on the wooden quayside in Argentina. That one last moment before breath left him and was replaced by blood or air. Was he thinking of her, his Mary Jane, his wife? Maybe no one really knows the dreams you have at death but had any of this occurred to her?

I wondered if his murderer also lay dozing in agony, awaiting his own fate before he himself fully awakens and has time to pray, before working, before falling in love, before dying in a strange new country. It was all a circle no matter how tragic or how sadly I mourned but then our lives are full of circles; and luck has shown me it doesn't always go your way. It was missing for the Bucko just now but that's just the time to gather yourself around you.

Maybe Mary Jane and I were both too close to the ones we loved most. The native Indians could do it in the Mid-West where their spirits had resided for thousands of years but not here in this city of else-where where everyone was from another place and had their own dreams, this city full of shadows and wild voices not unlike in its own way that same brown and unruly Argentina.

Mary Jane's marriage drew a red empire curtain across the story. I would have done more but then again; I wasn't allowed to. She wouldn't have me. Is it to him my brother then, that I should have been the protector, should have been there to keep the memory of his soul alive, but instead coveted his wife? I live with these broken commandments.

When she married, they returned to Burlington Street where the Butcher kept his shop. It was like going home and back up in the world for her. They made room for her son William who kept our George's name, and the Butcher would give provide safety just as Frank Clegg had provided for Mary Agnes even though their lives were boring, and they lived sedately across the water.

It was cold water on my face, but it was over and that was that. The Bucko erased the trace of any dreams under those cold, grey skies and likewise the remains of that thin fierce fiery face and eyes that burned like coals. Holy water on a face of stone, smooth and featureless and ready again to go to sea. It echoed all that had once been treasured. No golden coins for the Bucko now.

There was a time when she said to me. 'You haven't seen my ribbons Johnny and I don't want you to see them.'

She looked at me out of those liquid black, second generation famine eyes.

'Now I just want to have a sip of whisky, bring the kids up, be happy and forget about terrible events. What is wrong with that?'

Five

I joined the Booth Line a month later in late blue October, the year the Liberals won their famous election (1906) and all the men on our street who weren't away voted Irish Nationalist and I put my hands together and prayed for the sea to help the Bucko forget and set sail for the Atlantic port of Belem and the mighty Amazon.

Maggie Booths, they called the Line that took me there. Margaret the daughter, the scion of the family, lived in the rich quarried suburbs of the South end of the city. Her Uncle was one of the founders of the Salvation Army, Major William Booth, the one who declared of the waterfront communities that 'Communism was a necessity of their lives because economically they are worthless and morally, they are worse than worthless.' A nice feller that; the Mission padres full of his sort at the beginning of their tenure before they wise up.

I'd always wanted to taste Brazil. I loved Mary Jane. It took a while to forget her but if anywhere it would be on those dark and scented rivers. The bums on the Manhattan piers told me to go that way when I used to stumble around the Lower East Side and bummed rides to Central Park, chasing the shadows of my lost brother George.

'The Rio Negra that's the place you should be Buddy. The trees will carpet your loss.'

They had all been away from those crowded places at the bottom of the misty island, where Streets were listed in single numbers and the river fell away from them on the tangled piers of lower Manhattan, the same as in Liverpool. You would do anything, anything to get away especially if your heart has been broken and even if you're in the best city on earth, it doesn't mean a damn to the shattered lives of the poor.

From the time Mary Jane married her Butcher; nobody caught a glimpse of me for nigh on three years. They barely recognised the Bucko when he joined the same ship again, the *Lanfranc*, thirty-four months later. On the Amazon I swapped the life of the deck for one of the stokeholds on the river ferries down in that hell hole of what passes for an engine room. Beggars can't be choosers. These were places where the heat steams into blisters on your hands and the shovel somehow becomes part of you, flesh and metal together and your eyes are like the coals that are piled before you and are swept hissing like devils into the angry fire. All this to keep the paddle wheels turning on those ships with such little draw. A stoker and a would-be trader on this mystic river. God knows how those stokers of Marsh Lane, those firemen made it to cross the Western Ocean in five days.

Brazil was different. The opening of the Suez Canal might have transformed the world of shipping from Sail to Steam and reduced drastically the times of the passage from Europe to Australia but the difference between the bright deck and that furnace below was something different again. It seemed to reflect the sort of place it was, dark and furtive and explosive with secrets. It suited the Bucko just fine.

To get lost in that dense darkness isn't so bad if you want to hide away, if your heart has taken a pasting; what is worse in that fickle subterranean world is where the doubts creep in about what you could have done, doubts capable of penetrating any crack in your head, your body, or your soul. Say a Rosary.

Sweat rags can't mop away that mental torture. The helping hand you give your body might serve you well enough but the opening in your mind permits every dream, every seven bell breakfast, every constant infiltration to bring that darkness within you as if you wore a new mask every day; enough to peel away your eyes from the inside, the madness reaching down from within with all its smells of nothingness and fear.

In time you see it for what it is and even the most frightening scene becomes a place of calm but that's not how it was in the beginning on that twisting brown water nor on those double decker ferry boats that plied it, a place of calm and peace within a bubble of madness. If the engine room suited me very well, it was because it was dark and solitary and lost; a punishment on top of a punishment; a time for the Bucko to wrap that cape of good fortune around him.

'The poets of the sails,' my old man used to say, 'are the saviours of the ship.'

He was talking of the men that worked the deck. That wasn't the case for me anymore.

Coming into those small wooden wharfs, steaming through the brown heat, I gradually came to think I was in heaven amongst the stench and general fetidness of the soaked and sodden humidity, the overwhelming green; the constant rain, the sun and heat like a balm, a joy among the rubber planters and the natives, sitting on crates near the dock existing off coffee, bananas, and medicinal herbs; smells so strong they invaded you that you needed strong drink to settle you amongst this beauty and chaos; a warm, tropical Liverpool where stories are unending, it added to my dreams and made me want to say, hullo there, Bucko Johnny has landed his slot.

I did everything a seaman would do, something found within us in that beautiful lost green world. Before the ship lay at anchor off Belem, my world turned around food and drink and women and my self- pitying heart but there was something else here and I wanted to stay where slowly everything gets spun into talk and dreams between planters, the forest natives and seamen; spun into stories, the past breaking into the present like the breaking of an egg.

Something happened to me when those forests took me in, that river, that water, like a sculptor had embraced me, infused me with her breath of life, like a mistress had smiled impassively at me, somewhat amazed as she admired me, admiring her in all her perfection, her creation, she gazed and pointed the way for me to wrap myself around her, around the trees, the flowers, the water, her lovely plants. I forgot Mary Jane.

Until then I was still labouring under the illusion from the sayings off the boxcars and flat irons of the Mid-West that when a woman's husband dies, she marries his brother; like they did here, like the Native Americans did there. Why should I be surprised that it did not happen? I was a Gringo just like our poor George even if I was Liverpool Irish. Instead, the forest became my mistress and led me to others and found for me the blankets we wrap around us to hold in all our illusions and dreams, the flowers we make out of life, the wrap of our own good luck. I wasn't the Crazy Horse who always knew what he was doing until he walked into that trap.

I backed out of that Maggie Booth ship without a single thought the moment she landed at Manaus and settled in a cabin at the end of the far docks. When the ferry needed a fireman, I was first in line. It was there I first I met Maria Fidelia or Mariaste as they called her here, a child of the forest taught by itinerant Carmelite nuns.

BOOTH LINE, LIVERPOOL. R.M.S. "LANFRANC" (TWIN-SCREW), 6400 TONS.

THE LANFRANC

John Brown sailed to Brazil on her in 1906 and the same ship brought him home as a Distressed British Seaman In 1909 after he had spent almost three years working the ferries of the Rio Negra operating out of Manaus.

She came and stood next to me. I got scared. The sight and nearness of such a woman nearly paralysed me like I had taken a drug; maybe it was the shock of seeing her so suddenly like that, maybe it was my own confusion but in that instant the nearness of her and that crazy glassy glitter of her eyes made me want to jump up and press her close to me, hold her tight, rip her clothes off. I had to steady myself. I had just got this job and thrown in my lot with the river. It would be too much for me to go careening off now. Mariaste was known around these huts.

The feeling lasted only for a moment and was gone. She stared across the room with those dark eyes insolently watching me and I turned my face towards the wooden framed window, not so much worried by her insolence but about the feeling that had just gone through me like a knife. Now there was a scented fragrance in the hut and a smell that floated after her that had no right to be in the jungle. The whole episode made me nervous and uncertain.

'The Heliconia which you call Lobster Claw sustains us, would it sustain you?' Her eyes questioned me.

'Do you think that the rubber and the pink and yellow orchids will water you,' she said and rolled them again.

'The Giant Water Lily is one that could hold a man, that a man could lie upon.' She winked and gave a grin. She knew more about plants than any Botanist.

I started to ask her what she really wanted but she wasn't the kind to accept those sorts of questions. I got up off the chair and offered her the only piece of furniture in the hut apart from the bunk. My old storm lamp hung on a hook above the busted table. She looked at the chair and then at me thoughtfully, smiling her indifference in merely sitting down. She then went around the hut and looked at the pages of some makeshift journal I had been keeping, pasted on the logs.

'Rubbish,' she said.

'Just get out,' I said.

It was as though she had not heard me. She sat on the bunk and dangled her feet on the dirt floor.

'I love you,' she said. 'You're my man and tonight you are going to love me.'

I heard Nancy's word blowing up from the restaurant on those blue and white streets of 'Frisco except here it was dark, and you could hear animals crying from the jungle. Where was Nancy now? where was I now? So much for the Carmelites.

I said.' Some other time Lady, not tonight, I've had some hard days.'

The odour of the forest washed through her. She held out her long arms.

I'm so lonely, 'she said.

'Alright' I said, 'we'll just sit here and talk for a while.'

She smiled but it was with the eyes of a jaguar that knows every blade of grass, every broken twig along its path.

She held my hand and believe me I did all she said with the nights calling us and a million insects and birds singing in my head, and they brought a background to my dreams through the passion and fruit and the Bromeliads and Monkey Brush Vine, that grew around us in such profusion as we loved into the chattering and howling dark.

She lived through the week close to the cabins that

surrounded the ferry. Set back from the water amongst the trees. We grew close in those places. The Booth line was as far away from me now as the Liverpool I had sailed from. I sweated in the boiler room on those boats up and down the brown and green river and watched all of life grow around me, live, flourish and die. I would come back soaked and happy and sometimes a little drunk to sit in the cabin beside her; set back on its wooden stilts and the waters reflecting in the tin and cracked mirror on the wall. The Bucko sat back and watched while she brushed her lovely hair.

On Fridays she would take the money I gave her and purchase goods from the Chandlers store and return to her husband and children in a village on the other side of the water. The Iliad's burst around us and raged in different colours of blue and purple, red and orange leaves and when I awoke in afternoons in her arms before a night sailing, I would see them all arranged before me like a magical carpet. The passionflower and its fruit, the vine often seen hanging from the canopy of trees above us, all the soft and white, pink and purple flowers whose hearts look like paper came with an intricate smell that the Indians used with its leaves to act as a pain reliever and sedative for their dreams.

Many a night I chewed those strange bitter leaves with her head on my shoulder and the sounds of the forest echoing like a bell of all the fruit gathered inside and out and I sometimes felt like I was above the trees and could see, far in the distance, the sparkling ocean. We used its gentle fronds to treat any cough or fever and the sweats that are common here between such sunlight and the constant rain.

With these drugs, youth and life, age and death come quietly with the rhythm of the night and a peace settled over me, the peace of home, the peace of elsewhere among the seven hundred different types of trees. She taught me about these things as if I was an innocent. She treated those flowers as if they had lives just like us, like humans and she made me recognize too, the sound of a bird or a lynx on its silent rounds, then like them she would depart on the Friday or the morning of the week- end and return across the river.

The huge lilies store more liquid and food than any seafarer could drink and adapts its leaves to curve and overlap at their bases to form a tank of water. They can hold so many more pints of liquid than we could ever put away after a shift or even with my campanero's on a Saturday night when Mariaste was over the river. Working below on those ferries brings on a thirst like a waterfall the lilies were more than enough for me. But the passion fruit also brings you calm; the sweet sadness of absence; many a long weekend in the jungle I thought of Our George but little of my time with his widow. What was done was done.

The Indians say there is a cure for everything here except death. They insist on this until it is time that they themselves have to journey to the ancient lands. They sit and meditate under a tree and chew their drugs until they're gone from this earth, upon their last voyage, backs rubbed and succoured by the scented bark and not in the stench of some lousy courtyard off the Bootle dock road where the only luxury in the passing of some poor soul might be a flower, a candle, a clean sheet or a glass of whisky.

I learnt from these people. Their gods do not grant them re-incarnation, nor do the living beseech it for who would make of their Gods a liar ? Such peaceable souls, they truly do not know what death is except that their spirit must make another trip and that they can only accept that voyage with good grace.

Coffee plants, that grow up to 30 feet high carpet the tangled ground and it is beneath them that these living souls go to savour their last smell upon this earth.

The merchants may die in their bottles, their marble houses or for us seamen, the seraphim of the night, in the Missions that dot this river with their Benedictine and Carmelite priests but for the Indians they say the best way to pass over is amongst the trees and flowers and to join with all the other spirits of the forest. For us white men from the broken-down river districts, even if Catholicism is within our hearts , the passage is not so easy.

My buddies would have said I had gone native because I liked their ways here; those in Manhattan and on the long Melbourne piers would laugh at me now. It makes sense. They would have reached for the jug long ago but I am here and they are there and I know where I would prefer to be. The world here that the Indians live and cultivate under the huge shade of trees mixes with the spirits of their dead and living and bring a peace and solemnity, a daily source of rhythm to their lives. The Bucko wanted that rhythm in his own.

The passion flower is also often used in the great Catholic rituals that bless the church in the sunlight of their missions; upon the rock of Jerusalem they give to the poor of my parish the same as they give it here, but it does not afford as to the natives their beautiful death dream; their sweetness. Their medicine is like a permanent state of life and death to them. The shadow and sunlight of each new day comes in a hammock beneath the great canopy of the forest and includes the sweep and the floss of the stars you sometimes see like chinks of glass between the bunched and darkened twist of the trees. Their very soul lives within the haze of this forest, not under some wide sky or upon some rolling sea nor crammed into the blackened courts that line the Liverpool river.

I chew the gum Maria Fidela gives me, some call it sapodilla, others chicle, and stretch my back against the bark , the Indians say it is always good to stretch before a journey, and smell the fruit and stench of the forest, the time comes and goes and I try to search for my spirit, the spirit that always clings to you no matter how hard you seek to capture its essence or ignore it. The Indians say if you are lazy it goes to someone else, or just when you have left sitting or have sat too long, along it comes in such an unforeseen form, that it is not possible to hold onto or to prove or to show. It is like an after shadow of the sun. Sometimes it is gone long before you, its grace never given.

When I am not working I come to this spot each day to sit with Maria among the thousand different flowering plants. She gives names to all the trees that can be found in one small square around us. She says, with her lovely hair, black as the scented wood, there is before you a whole a circle of life of which the teachings of the church is unaware.

'Here in the Forest in the Amazon. The plants depend on the animals and the animals depend on the plants for food and shelter and we too are full of circles.'

'And who depends on us?' The Bucko asks.

She is all spirit and laughter and disappears with her visions.

I am none the wiser between the natives, the outsiders, and the ships out at sea on the wide Atlantic but I acknowledge her deep knowledge and her strong brown shoulders as she expertly paddles a skiff full of bundles to the other shore. She tells me she'll see me on Monday, her husband, and children are waiting for her now.

I try to find my place, the only place made for me, where each part of me is protected, where every part of you is loved, but I could search forever here and not feel that sense of peace. That is the problem with peace you always want more of it. Indeed, you could search every leaf, every tree every flower but still might not find it. How many mornings would I wake exhausted from trying to forge its passage? Here, life sometimes more closely resembles death, both paradise and death, one disguised as the other. Mariaste would never really know me just as I would not fully know her.

The one they call Master, one of the elders says to me,

'You will flourish and maybe find love here, but you will not win your life. It is far from this forest. You will never fall asleep with such dreams as ours to carry you even if this place was yours forever.'

He accepted my money with a solemn and decorous nod. He was not fooling. No matter what great comforts this place brought me, neither the variety of colours nor places that only the special birds with their magical beaks can reach would truly console me. Neither the Coco Plant or the White Trillium Flower, Trumpet Tree and Castor Beans; nor the Heliconia flower which Maria Fidela first taught me to love, nor the flower of her own beautiful being could ultimately sustain me.

He said, 'We also call it Wild Plantain, Parrot Flower and False Bird of Paradise, but in each name, we see its image in a different light.'

The Master quietly turned and spoke. 'This is not your place; this is not for you, this false paradise. Everything is found here, everything they use for many types of medicine but it will not cure you. This is not your place; you need the sky and the sea not this carpet of rotten wood that we love and nurture and immerse ourselves within its ordure.'

'*A despedida*' he said.

He was warning me away; warning me before I too caught the sickness of disillusionment and desolation and finished staying on living out of a bottle and a hammock, unshaven crumpled and dirty vested like many of the white traders; a sticky glass instead of all the beauty that had originally filled their souls. It was like a dream, and I felt as if I had been dreaming, that my dream had lasted for years. In many ways it had. But the Bucko also knew what he was telling me was true.

One of the rich traders sought a conversion to the faith from a Catholic priest that often visited our settlement. He invited him to his house to eat. He also invited me as I had drunk with him before on many a Saturday night.

'Ah but you have to make the long spiritual journey,' the father was saying, 'it is not a simple process to merely enter tout suite.'

He spoke in a vigorous manner the way all Jesuits do when they are solicited, eating and drinking but he chose his words carefully and his hands became still, the same as what was before him on the plate and in his glass.

'Of course,' he said very softly as if he was speaking of something better left unsaid.

'There is in the special cases of the religious mature, another passage.'

'Certainly Father, the shorter version please,' the trader said.

He'd lived on this river for too long not to understand a few things appertaining to the bargains of the soul.

'Where you can roll all of the sacred mysteries together, Baptism, Confirmation, Communion – all done by Noon,' he added.

He didn't say that we could then all get back here for a good drink, but the priest looked at him with steel hardened eyes as if something needed to be rectified.

'Of course, my son, special measures call for special offerings on the part of the Penitent.'

'Of course, Father, of course.'

It was just the trader's way of reaching for another insurance policy in what he called this flyblown heap where he had made his money but where death could approach at any moment and didn't need an appointment. The Bucko had come here broken hearted but was now leaving with a sense of ease, maybe he also needed that insurance policy but not one to keep him hiding here amongst the trees.

The last month of my wages, I gave to Maria Fidela and kissed her goodbye. We both knew what lay between us.

I left the forest and worked my way back downriver to Belem. The crew on the ferry knew I would leave, and some gave me money to exist on the quayside until a ship came to that city of water and bells and white Atlantic Light.

I used to think that my heart lay in this forest but that old master was right, the Bucko was not young anymore but at the age of forty-three (1909) and nearly three years under the cover of deep foliage and the great friendship of a woman he had loved he knew this age would stay within him but needed to leave it. The first glimpse of the sea told him he was right, his home was elsewhere.

I hung around the wharves, got to know the right gangs and waited for my passage. The Dockers here say that the devil himself tries to adopt the form of a nanny goat or a great black dog for anyone who tries to escape the jungle. Sometimes you can see him sat on a bollard: also, that a strong smell of Sulphur tends to announce his appearance on the wind that blows over from the forest, never the sea, he hates the open spaces. He knows his place.

Even in his human form he tends to wear a long pigtail and cloven shoes. The docks clear when that smell blows down the quayside. The Indians of the million trees are no different; they have their own comforting rumours against evil spirits just like the Catholics have theirs. I looked at my feet with great relief and waited for a ship.

Six

Maggie Booth's signed the Bucko on again, worked him half to death and still registered me as a Distressed British Seaman (1909) so the company could collect their money from the Board of Trade. No one speaks well of Maggie, of her company, of her loyalty, of her tastes. There was many a seaman who would never enter her folded arms for fearing being in more debt leaving the ship than they entered three months before.

Her captains fined (logged) ferociously anyone missing in port, any time lapses aboard, any missed watches, fearsome debt collections, prohibited uses of alcohol, excessive drink and other general deductions, it was if her old uncle was waving his Salvation Army baton in fury at the Amazon's exotic allure. All took their toll on the ship's company of wretched seafarers. If you want to make someone worse, like the Army, hit him harder.

Maggie herself could have been registered to one of the Gin Palaces on Paradise Street and probably was, with the sailors of fifty years ago. No wonder her uncle was such a scion of probity with his excoriations of the life lived in dockland communities. The company got money for me, for bringing me home, but as they provided both me and the State a service, I received no wages.

They brought me back aboard the very ship the *Lanfranc* I had sailed on here three years before. The Bucko was coming home but I knew in my heart I would go away again for good. I had rejected too many things and embraced too many others to know within myself what was going on.

In Kirkdale I stayed again with Francis James and his wife Rose who was a kindly soul with a sweet smiling face. Billy and Nelly were going so hard through the motions that they still didn't want anything to disturb them. At the house on Wolsey Street where Francis James and Rose lived the place was swimming with kids. Alice, Rose's sister lived next door and their place was battered with them as well but as usual they still made a place for me.

'It's too late for us,' Nelly would scream.

Billy five years older would try to sooth her. Her father and sister downstairs on Othello Street told her to keep quiet. They liked Billy. My Mary Jane the one who had rejected me was popping kids out every two years since she'd married her Butcher. Every month

brought news of a new tragedy from Nelly's doorstep
no matter how many shifts Billy missed at the Canada
or Brocklebank docks, trying to time the tides of his
wife's ovulation.

My brother Francis James was born in the same slum
tenement as all the other boys. Two   years separated
him from Billy and the same two years later Henry
was the last born in 1878, the baby of the family, those
triple biennials that added three sons and great exhaustion to our Ma, no wonder she looked worn out.

Rose looked after us all and was backed up by her
sister Alice, her docker husband Edward Williams and
their six children in the house next door in the streets
the Welsh developers had built all along Wolsey and
the rest of the Shakespeare streets towards the turn
of the Century.

For a housepainter Francis James had very small hands
as though he could have been an engraver or a fine
artist. When he was little about five or six, me and the
Da used to tease him ; we used to tell him, life is like
a billowing sail and in its layered folds it will spread
before you all of your options. You could become a
captain or an engineer, a boxer, a writer or a painter
but as time passes with every choice, every turn of

the wind, the sail will roll and point you to a single direction, until it converts into a single strand, a furled one sheeter horizontal and solitary at the mast. You will become a seaman or a docker; then we'd laugh.

'Don't be cruel to him,' the Ma would shout.

Maybe he heard us too well because Francis James stayed a house painter for a quarter of a century and never left Wolsey Street until he went to war and when he went to that war maybe he was thinking of wharves and ships and quaysides that his brothers had visited all over the world. It was a pity he chose that for his adventure. For instead of coming back to our district a hero, he was killed in a different set of Sandhills running the length of that part of eastern France and the tiny Belgian coastline. Killed in similar dunes he once used to roam with his own kids on the grassy sands that spun out from our stretch of the river above Seaforth, that now became his graveyard on the far side of the La Manche.

He married Rose Smith in 1900 and had eight children with her before the machine guns cut him to pieces in the November of 1917. Both Rose and her sister Alice were born and raised on Pelops Street, another of the Shakey's, just up the road from St Alexander's;

but it was on Wolsey Street that both sisters, Francis and Edward Williams started to establish their own dynasty.

Francis began his married life one door down to the river and next door the other side of Rose's older sister and her family at number 24. When number 20 became available they took it straight away and moved to the main side of Stanley Road that followed Scotland Road as the main highway through the North end and out of the city.

It was a bigger house. They needed it for future kids but it meant there was space for me when I came home and before more children came along to occupy it like baby Alice in 1908 and young Rose in 1910 and while little Mary was still sleeping in a cot in her mother and father's room from 1912, the eldest Edward James was set up in the attic and Georgina tucked away somewhere behind a settee. They had lost Florence in 1904 and young Francis in 1906 and John was yet to be born in 1918 three months after his father's death in Western Flanders.

I used to love to see our Francis walking with the younger ones, the baby in a pram, to the station at Bank Hall and catch the electric train four stops to

Waterloo where they would play in our sandhill's that rose up from the beach, all the way along the river to Formby point and the waiting ships on the Mersey bar which separated it from the Irish Sea.

The *Lanfranc* that brought me home was a good ship but, and even if they got their worth out of me, that sad Maggie Booth still had my book marked with a Distressed British Seaman stamp and I had to ship out again to clear my name.

The Federation was forever trying to clamp down on the number of those backing out of ships especially from Liverpool and to clear that stamp, they wanted you deep sea again and fast. But seamen could not help jumping ships. In the Americas and the Antipodes the temptations were too great and we felt it was our right. Money, Food or Women always held sway, drink was a given, but the Bucko was moving somewhere else beyond ships or bricks and even passed Liverpool, the somewhere else city.

Rose Smith, our Franny's wife was a good soul. She was born in the same year as our Henry and Billy's Nelly so there were always birthdays in that house. She and her sister Alice who was born in the same year as Francis James were daughters of James Schmidt a German Sailor from Heligoland who changed his name to Smith when he settled in these tight streets and married an Irishwoman from an old Roscommon family, Sarah Curtis whose father had died at the fever sheds on Great Howard Street and left a legacy of weak lungs within the family. No wonder Mary Jane wanted away for herself and her son.

Apart from being very motherly Rose was a big friendly woman who always seemed to wear a steady dancing smile, but everyone knew what the deaths of the two children Florence and Francis had cost her. They also knew that she would have more children, many more, and that in its own way added to Nelly's suffering.

Liverpool was many cities in those days with streets and alleys and parishes tucked in behind the docks that were like their own little towns. Streets that were often embattled and even packed houses in noisy thoroughfares might well have had a moat around them such were the dynasties inside. Having two sisters with their own large families living side by side to each other, created a collective ring, a freedom in numbers on Wolsey Street. There might be a housepainter and a docker as nominal heads of households for Census purposes but alongside these two strong women nothing came between them; decision making, cooking or organizing, men were the second front. The sisters' mother died when they were young, and they were used to looking after and taking control.

Number 20 Wolsey Street was a rambling maze and in each room, with the kids lying around on chairs or beds, or couches with the stuffing and springs hammered out of them or some old relative from Ireland or Germany sitting down drinking tea, there was always something lying in wait for you, a reminder of other times. If the chalk drawings you saw the kids scribble on the wall came to life or in the kitchen where your dead brother's lips dripped blood onto the tattered fabric of the tablecloth or rosary beads on your father's old chair you felt the memories rise up inside like pins. Was there enough of us here to dampen the shadows?

Scary stuff if you worried too much about it; Amelia, my sister on the other side of Mary Agnes, the first death I had known when I was five and our George just being born in the Northern Hospital and look where he is now in an early grave on the Argentine.

'Don't let it bother you,' my Ma said, 'Around here birth and death is every woman's nightmare.' Maybe she was also going a little crazy in her own quiet way.

The Bucko thought that's what these streets did to you.

Sometimes he wonders if we don't all have creases in our life like the folds of an accordion or the Macassar laid over a chair, a couch where stuff falls down somewhere and lasts from another age and only gets shaken out when things jolt you like someone dying and leaving this earth; you discover that each time is maybe different but there is still a continuous line running through you like the Indians or the Catholics believe in their own way. Something outside history and to do with circles, maybe that allays the horrible dreams but when you have witnessed death as a kid in those dark places then as a man what are you supposed to feel?

Maybe I brought a different gaze, a new truth when I came down the plank of the *Lanfranc* my head held high even as someone so called *distressed* a displaced seaman but that did not worry me; you grow up and afterwards you get old and think about what you could have and would have done and try to separate those things you can do nothing about but there is always something inside you nagging away, a fidgety restlessness that had to lead somewhere.

For now, it was in the thought of making a new home as much inside me as outside that obsessed me, beyond our old house, that slum, that midden, my Ma kept as clean as she could keep but there is always stuff rising before us that is still part of our frightened dreams. They only disappear when we started work – and after we leave it; always the work where both dreams and nightmares get lost or battened down by routine or fatigue, the Bucko wanted more than that.

I don't know why the house on Wolsey Street made me feel this way because, it was always full of laughter and singing and Francis James and Rose were happy and so were the kids, except poor Edward who suffered from the time he was born with a bad chest but sometimes those creases opened up inside me and despite all the loving care around could not seem to compensate. Bucko Johnny was laughing but always with that something else buried inside him.

'You're just gloomy,' Francis James told me, 'You've spent too much time under the shadow of those trees. You need to get out into the light.'

I stayed with them for nearly six months. To go back deep sea, I had to clear my name with the Federation. I did some short trips around the coast, to Ireland and to France like I did when I stayed with Billy and Nelly more than six years before but that did not cut the mustard with the Federation bosses. They wanted you back on the long jags to properly clear your book.

It was my brother Henry, the youngest, more than ten years younger than me, the baby, that got me to think about Aussie again; the brother whose wedding I had not attended out of stupid religious spite. In some ways he was glad we did not go there to the Everton Valley because there was no drink and because Catherine was so young, a slight tut tut tut hung in the air. It did not make me feel any better. I should have gone. My brothers said the same, to no one in particular or anyone within earshot at the bar, but they blamed me, I was the eldest, Liverpool was that sort of place.

'A trip down to there would clear you Johnny,' Henry said in his quiet strong voice. He was very similar to Francis James in build, tall but slightly slimmer and with a very good manner about him, easy and reasonable and a cogent arguer of his point of view.

He did not mean forever, but I knew by then something had changed within me too.

He had just come off the White Star ship the *Afric* which despite her name ran on a regular six month run to the Australian coast. Knowing my history, he said he didn't want me to join it yet because he knew that ship could be useful later as he could always get me aboard. He was well known upon her.

He was proved right. Like in the many ways he did business it was the right decision, the right order of things, maybe living all that time with the Protestants up in Saint Domingo gave him more of a cutting edge when it came to decisions. He acted like a Lutheran Catholic and applied a Cartesian logic to every situation.

During this time Our Ma wasn't great, I became worried. This is where his wisdom came into play. He hadn't seen her for some time, being away and didn't know she now lived in an attic room on the other side of Stanley Road.

'What's the problem?' he said.

'I'm sure she's sick and I don't know what to do.' I said.

'What's wrong with her?' he asked.

'Her mind is all wrong. She acts as if she's not there.'

'What does she do?'

'She does crazy things, gets people's names wrong, streets, families, kids all mixed up.'

'Does she comb her hair?'

'What?'

'I said does she comb her hair?'

I shook my head, what sort of question was that?

'As long as a woman combs her hair you don't have to worry,' he said.

'Since I've been home, she combs it. 'I said.

'Well then maybe it's not so bad,' he said.

'I'll go around and see her.'

With his guidance, I joined the ship the *Brodholme*, later to become part of the Blue Star Company for another long trip down to the great south land. The ship was good, and I was looking forward to going down again to Aussie. She was a fine ship with a good crew and after eight weeks at sea we jibbed Fremantle and berthed in Albany on the western edge of the

Great Bight. I jumped again of course. Fuck the Federation, this was one of a seaman's sacred freedoms and seeing this was my second time in Aussie in nearly twenty-five years, I wanted to see more of the country under my own steam.

The Bucko liked it then and he liked it even better now. I hitched on an old grain truck with battered sides and a roaring engine on the road from Albany to Esperance where the wind blows cooler and signed on straight away as a Fireman (Australian Merchant Navy Records) on a small coaster and instead of clearing my stained British record, I made it worse, but it was what the medicine man said I had to do, to find, to properly live, to be alive. It was what I thought anyway. Below me the sea glowed transparent with light, sometimes it twitched as though a vast vaporous cloth had been thrown over it where the blue sparkled through. The Bucko had his own mind, it was clear to me now.

Crazy horse or Bucko Johnny, it was all the same in the purple light of the West. I stayed away from the drink; anywhere without a drink was hard in Aussie then, but berths were also hard to find so I laid low and kept my coastal wages.

Going around those small southern piers on a little ship taking general cargo, the down below crowd and other men I worked with thought I was some sort of solitary or an inhabitant of New Zealand.

'Does the hermit get bored,' they'd shout after a shift?

'It's not so easy to bathe in grease,' I'd shout back even though there was only two feet between us.

Behind us was all the vast swell of the Southern Ocean. I always loved that big light that stretched to the bottom of this earth, sometimes on deck, I'd watch the clouds and think this is what this life has brought me. I haven't wasted my years, searching for forgotten flowers, bathing in unresisted pleasure, in attempted happiness, making others happy, to keep happy myself? I was in good company. If you traveled far enough south from here you would see icebergs, large floating mountains like white prisons and the immense black and blue of the sea crumpled around them but floating free.

What is old and beautiful in the forest turns and blows away like dust in this great wide-open land. Sometimes I feel like singing. Sometimes a man like the Bucko can seek solitude as deep as the folded canopy of the rainforest but it is in the open spaces or near the sea, he comes alive, a jolt of joy from any one unknown moment to the next. Anyone in the world can play my tune. If you know you have your own song somewhere deep inside, you; then you can happily join the crowded wharfs.

One evening just three days after Christmas while the rest of the crew were eating pork chops, drinking, raging and fighting, I went to my usual spot to sit quietly on the silent Well deck and found it occupied: the same two of them there, in stokehold rags and drinking cider. They invited me over. The sea was the colour of pearl with orange and yellow scratch marks across the far sky.

'You might be strange, but you can still have a drink' they said.

It was better than before when one of them said,

'You've got a face on you like boiled piss mate.'

He shot jets of smoke from the corner of his mouth, his cigarette dangling, he looked at the sky as if the oncoming stars would bring him truth instead of the stokehold where he'd labored half his life. I laughed but then I started to cry. It was just the anniversary in the same brown and orange hemisphere that the knife pierced our George's heart and put out such a young laughing life.

'It's all right mate,' they said, 'you have a good bucket,' they knew there was something up with me, some sad memory. I gazed over to the shoreline, the tide rolling in, the sun hung on the rim of the sea, its last rays gilded and softened the rocks where green combers seethed and foamed. A line of red seemed to have descended and be running through the spray. George would have loved it here. They were good spirits; it was his blood.

Later that year in 1910 (Crew Lists) I'm into my stride and aboard a bigger Aussie ship The *Kanowna* a pleasure steamer out of Fremantle and one of the first honorary liners of the Australian Steam Navigation Company, shipping passengers from the West to Sydney, via Port Adelaide, Albany, Esperance and Melbourne. I loved it, good food, good pay; I knew where I was. I was liked. I had a new book, a shiny green Australian one, a new union, I stayed on her; my new truth was working.

Between these different ports, I sailed for three years and travelled all those windy coastlines, tranquil and serene. The *Kanowa* was built in Dumbarton Scotland for the Aussies who were starting to take an interest in their own ports of their vast windy continent. She was regular to Fremantle, and she paid well. Freo was my home now, I had stayed in the Mission often enough but in the finish, I had a little cabin of my own near Kwinana beach and could sit out there at nights and watch the sky and the water and know I was earning well and could send money home regular without it killing me.

Thinking back on it now, it was Our Henry, that tall laconic soul who was the architect that paved this path for me, his practicality and my own visions made for a happy combination. Easy going Henry in those sunlit streets of our home in summer, a quietness about him but with a purpose to his walk that made people look when they saw him coming. He was the one that gave me the push, the one that made the decision easy by singling out that one ship as an insurance policy. He was a deep one my youngest brother even in one so young; the one who got me going south again after so many years because he knew how it suited me.

THE KANOWA

An Australian Merchant Navy cargo liner originally built for Australians to enjoy their own coastline. John Brown's time aboard her was a happy one. He stayed for many years on one of the first ships of the Australian Steam Navigation Company

Henry left those miserable tight little cobblestoned streets off Saint Domingo Road and brought his wife and child back down closer to the water. He made sure the old lady could keep an eye on them and he could keep an eye on her as well by way of making her less crazy. He sailed out aboard the *Afric* on regular six-month jags. No one in our family thought he would go to sea, but he did and stayed for five years until he had some money behind him and then went back on the docks. He hardly took a drink except water which his father-in-law, the Carter Benjamin Naylor called Adam's ale. He learnt a lot from his wife's parents, but it didn't make him any the lesser for that.

He was able to get a place of his own, closer to us, on Smith Street for himself, Catherine and the baby, young Catherine, who wasn't a baby anymore but had reached double figures by the time he packed it in and went back to the Canada dock when I saw him last.

He went back as a porter to the dock he'd worked before. There would always be a place for him there, but he had so many friends on that White Star ship and in that company because he always conducted himself well and was equally respected as a fighter for seamen's rights. I had only to mention his name and they would get me stowed aboard either back to

Liverpool or out again to Aussie anytime I needed.

Strange really it was the same ship, the *Afric* that transported our Billy down to South Africa when she was
used for carrying troops to the Boer war, that employed
our Henry in the stokehold and brought him nice
and easy back and forth to Liverpool all those years,
a respected fighter for the Union. It was the same
for me making the return journey. You could go into
any pub on Marsh Lane and mention his name and
someone would give you a nod or look after you and
you wouldn't need any shipping office to sign you up
as long as you had some money in your pocket.

I came back that way in 1913, just the way Henry said
I should, to see our mother, our Francis, the additions
to his family and Henry and his daughter Catherine,
who was now thirteen, Billy and Nelly. I wanted to see
them all. They liked me so much aboard the *Afric* of
the White Star Line that I returned to Aussie on her
as a regularly paid fireman some months later after I
had paid my respects to Wolsey, Orlando and Othello
streets; our very own *Shakey's* as the kids called them.

Homecoming was a bit like that year of all the mar-
riages out of our house in1900; it just lets you stay long
enough to know when to leave. I had heard enough

Tom Toms going off across Europe and I wanted no part of that game. Either the rising of the workers across every border would win what was rightfully theirs or another war would come our way. I knew where my money lay.

That last trip was great. Rushing to make the tide the *Afric* got stuck on a sandbank after leaving the dock, just below our house in that misty light of late November. As she was beginning her outward run into the river, she ran aground and became firmly stuck just opposite the streets from where we all lived. After several unsuccessful attempts to free her, her cargo was eventually lifted ashore, and she was pulled away by three tugs riding at high tide. Barges ferrying backwards and forwards and rocking in the swell brought her cargo back to the quayside. Reloading took days and days.

I was on the ship but used to hop ashore at night on the gig boats. We were on Board of Trade wages but apart from maintenance there were no boilers to be fired. It was great while it lasted, home every night, in your house for tea and then a drink in the Banjo. But when I left Liverpool that year, I could somehow smell the fates. The excitement in the air tells you all you need to know about the loud Jingo and the stench of death that always soon follows. Thickening mist on the river where the ship lay, fog spirals writhed, the air thickens and that other world disappears down a funnel leaving only wet sand on the banks, smothered by waters and the muffled call of a foghorn that could have been a drum in the belt of that winter of 1913.

It was the last time I saw any of them again.

Oh, I heard later of course, how the war took Francis James and my Ma just after with the Spanish Flu and a broken heart and poor sick Edward, Rose's eldest son in 1923. Three years later Rose's sister Alice lost her husband Edward Williams who died on the dock after unloading an infected cargo of Hides. Did all life still seemed settled at numbers 20 and 22 Wolsey Street with so many footings gone from those foundations?

And how Billy and Nelly took Rose's last baby from our Francis's house in the last year of the war. She had another five kids to look after including Edward who had been sick from birth, and it was hard for her emotionally and physically with Francis James gone. Nelly and Billy had been trying for years and years and knew they would never have another chance, so the child was passed over. They took him, the last boy in a family of girls, with Rose's blessing, and named him John after me the Bucko and moved away down river to the Welsh Streets just off Marsh Lane, Bootle to avoid the rattle of any neighborhood gossip that had so plagued Mary Agnes in our Courts.

I left the *Afric* for good when we got back down to Fremantle, and I became a regular Aussie as part of my third and final sojourn there. I had two Seaman's Discharge books now, better than any passport, one bright shiny and new from the Australia dominion and the Board of Trade duster that was shot through with holes and misdemeanors and crimes of which the British State had accused me. I was back home. That ship had served me well just as she had served our Henry. I threw the old book overboard somewhere between Adelaide and Sydney. Threw it away over the Southern Ocean as far as I could throw it, its loss leaving me like water flowing freely from a broken hull. A rim of light flooded up and nearly drowned me and I can still see those old pages rippling out, spinning off through the blue air, over blue water: history.

Between the Septembers 1914 – 1916, I worked the Darwin, Broom, Fremantle, Adelaide, Melbourne, Sydney and Brisbane run. I was an Aussie now. The *Indurra* was a great ship, a bigger ship than the *Kanowna* and built for the same expanding tourist base but double her size, all white infrastructure and sprung wooden decks. She looked a treat with the Aussie trade continuing to grow and the talk of more and more of her people taking trips around their own coastline and often docking in the eighteen ports that dotted their forgotten West.

I had a happy time on her though we did have to revolt once in 1914 when we were working as a troop ship bound for the Dardanelles. They would not give us extra drinking water when we were going through the tropics. The soldiers supported us. Under blood red skies we had them cheering when we straggled up to sit on the deck and the ship started to wallow in the water. After an hour or so, her iron hull started to softly drift against the slate blue sea; the heat dripping from every stanchion of her iron deck; a troopship without an engine or a soul.

The soldier's support gave us a welcome boost because the officers and captains and mates were either going to put us in irons or shoot us, but this was how their opposite number, the democratic, narky, Aussies did things. They cheered again.

It still makes me laugh. They would have hung us or transported us a century earlier if we had done that in England. None of the Aussie troops, all of them volunteers, would take a turn below despite the officers' exhortations and desperate pleadings. We got our extra rations, but God rest those poor souls later disembarking in flimsy landing craft on waters that ran with their blood.

My new life was now Johnny Brown Wailey a citizen of down under and this was the place, and these were the ships of the Aussie Steam Navigation Company that made me most happy for the next 15 years. Yes, the Bucko was happy enough, a few little drinks here and there, the staying in the Mission until the cabin was all fixed up, then the parties and good food and even a walk out now and then with one of the girls who ran the bar across the way.

Aussie was good to me. I nearly got hitched, old as I was but I thought it was more for pity than love, but the real pity was when the Company said they were going to have to retire me. It was policy since the war. You had to go at 65 fit or not. The year was 1931. I had a few more months. Here I was an old seafarer on a ship like a thousand others I had sailed in but when there are no temptations you get bored; when life is good you get shiftless. I was glad I was going in some ways, at other times totally disconsolate but the

Bucko would always find a path, he had that cape of good fortune wrapped around him.

I am not always bathed in grace, not always approaching the light. Sometimes when I would be sitting on deck by the galley door, I'd watch the shape of the clouds arrange themselves like golden threads across the sky and think of other times, other ships, other lives of the Bucko. Who isn't given to wonder sometimes?

There are no wasted years, just like ships, journeys to carry you from place to place, I'd learned that from the Indians of the forest. You need that wisdom when people start to disappear from your life. Sometimes it becomes hard to avoid the waste, the waste that life can bring or leave its taste but with two brothers lying in their graves so far away, it is never a good sign to dwell on. The Bucko did not dwell but he noted the feelings inside.

Life is beautiful and fragrant and precious and just because I am not young, I am still not soiled with it and have no great urge to weep but to laugh and resist. Resisting is the thing I have learned to do best. It is what middleweights wear on their boxing vests, the resistance of each stretch in the stokehold, and I tell myself I have come through this and in reality I am happy and in this passing is how I occupy myself, congratulating myself on my own good luck. The only time you miss the sea is when you are not on it but neither water nor bricks confine me now. All is good and everything comes to pass; other little things inside me sustain the Bucko.

But they said, 'When your birthday comes around this time Johnny; go and sit outside your cabin and enjoy the Ocean.'

Seven

That same year, some months before the company announcement and thirteen years after the end of the great war and all its sad aftermath of crutches and support trusses, oxygen masks and pushchairs parked outside many a front door leading to Freo Harbour, the Bucko is suddenly made a hero as if that fiasco has not taken place, has nothing to do with him anywhere along these sad antipodean shores.

The Perth and Fremantle newspapers have enlisted me as one great heroic soul as if that conflict rested only with the dead they buried overseas. Oh yes, they made a big potato out of Johnny Brown those papers. They said I'd rescued a young couple from drowning; as an honest fisherman, a loyal subject of King and Empire, a newcomer to this country instead of a sweat blasted member of the black gang, a Liverpool Irish Republican who had rocked around their coastline for the past twenty years; a seafarer to these golden ports for more than four decades in my three sojourns to this great and lonely land, a bloody fisherman! The real reason I was on that water, not a sea mile from my cabin, was that I was looking for the body of Rita Acello.

Gusty Cain first introduced me to her some months before I came off my last big jag. They knew Rita around the Mission. She drank and she smoked a lot of marijuana, Mary Jane, they called it here as if that wasn't enough of a laugh but I didn't care. The Amazon had taught me what medicine could do for the soul. But this was rough stuff. You could always tell by the smell of her clothes. They said she was 32 years old. I found out later she was much younger; another casualty of that great conflict or fiasco that came to us from that Europe across the water.

When she first approached me, I didn't get up but sat still, took a long breath and finally looked at her again. Her nose was pudgy, and her eyes spoke of hard nights, but she was not ugly and had rather heavy lips without rouge, they were pinkish and made for kissing but what got me were her eyes, their brilliance, their animalism and their recklessness, they glistened like swords, black pools that you could dive into. God knows what she had taken but she had smitten me, the Bucko.

'Kiss me,' she said with a laugh.

'Let's have a drink first,' I said.

'You use that cheap stuff they call Gold Dust?' I asked.

'Once in a while,' she said, 'when I'm tired.'

'It'll kill you,' I said 'why don't you get something better.'

She touched her pockets and crossed her heart.

'When I find my sailor,' she said.

I'd been in the forecastle too long and ducked and dived every trip of the way to get too swayed by that, but she had crept up on me with those eyes. It was always the same with the Bucko. Get out!! My insides screamed. My Aussie discharge book was now as clean as a whistle where before it was as ragged as a piece of salt beef with all the British Board of Trade 'decline to report' stamps across it. I was glad I had chucked *it* to the ocean.

'Kiss me,' she said again.

I said, 'how about that drink.'

She clenched her teeth.

'You think you know about me?' she said.

She pushed her hair back to reveal a high intelligent forehead, but it was the eyes that still held me.

'You're like the rest of them. You think you know about me here and that's why you won't kiss me because I disgust you.'

I thought she's crazy, I've got to get out of here, even the Padre was looking over. She leaned across me and held my mouth with her lips, her mouth tasting of the afternoon's liquor. She sat back, shaking with relief. I took out my white cotton handkerchief and wiped the sweat off my forehead. I could hear muffled laughter from the far corner of the room where the bums used to gather, slow, gurgling laughter like the sound of a small stream. She acted as if she wanted to pull me down in front of them.

'Let's go,' I said. I felt like a molester. And now she's sitting next to me in a bar and she's laughing even more now that she's kissed me. I am not a funny man and Bucko Johnny can be as melancholy as the rest of them, look as sad as at any lament, cry with the best but I'm making a young woman laugh? The Bucko feels good.

In another bar she fell on her knees before me and begged me to tell her she was not disgusting.

'Tell me.' She sobbed, 'Tell me I am beautiful like other women.'

'Of course, you are. You are really very beautiful,' I said. The bottle passed between us, golden light glinting on the thick glass and she sobbed as she drank and told old stories.

I tried to lift her spirits, but she was down in the depths way beyond anything I could do. I kept on trying old as I was, but she was gone. She was twenty- five.

I was earning good money going up and down the West coast from Darwen to Albany and every little port in between. We spent some time together, but it was mainly through drink and when I stayed at the Mission.

But she was cunning too. One day she told me to come with her. She ducked around a corner and continued for two streets until we came to an alley. She turned down it a couple of paces until she came to opening in the wall. Inside the darkened house there were people with faces that looked like the dead. The rooms inside rocked with smoke and swirled around and nearly choked me; it was almost pitch black and the smoke was like an astringent on my eyes; it leaped and danced around me and made me as blind as the people slumped against the walls like that infirmary on Third Street, New York. They looked as if they had been struck with some biblical sword and either slumped or lay where they had fallen like broken dolls or souls awaiting purgatory.

Rita rummaged in her bag for something forgotten or nonexistent.

'He's got the money.' She nodded behind her.

I paid and she picked up a package from some big Joey with dark skin.

'They're all Italians that run it,' she said. 'The boss is the grandson of a Calabrian who came here off the goldrush seventy years ago.'

'They seem to know you,' I said.

'They know me,' she said but she spat the words out as if they were stones.

My cabin in Kwinana was all set up. I'd paid it off from the good wages I was bringing home; many a time it lay empty. When I was on the short trips,

I'd stay at the Mission and take a drink and a bunk there. Sometimes we were only at the quayside for thirty hours but little by little Rita came to visit and sometimes stayed.

One time I even went to her home. It was a sick building, diseased by the sun and close to the water; the black pockmarked stone looked as if it had been built by someone who had made money right out of that first 'rush; now it was falling down, old and tired, a dust filled shell. She lived in a room; there was a camp bed, a radio and some dirty overstuffed furniture, the floor was littered with crumbs and balls of dust; the bed was down, and the sheets looked as if they had been well used.

There was a reproduction of the Blue Woman on one wall and on another a print of a young Aboriginal boy saluting the sky near Ayers rock. You could smell the garbage rising up from the kitchen and next to the cold larder was a tin of condensed milk and a pat of butter that had melted. Clothes lay in scattered piles on the floor behind the divan. Before the war, her family had travelled twelve thousand miles to find the hope of a great new life down here in the sunlight of the free. She had found this.

This was where she lived; I'd laughed with her at the mission; bought her drink and encouraged her to come to Kwinana whenever she wanted but she'd never brought me home before. I smelled it, touched it with my fingers, walked through it with my feet. It was as I imagined it but I was old now and she was young.

This was her home. Blindfolded the Bucko would have found the place, her odour, the cheap perfume possessed it, her fevered lost existence, when she should have been running the hills, exploring the Snowy Mountains, swimming the peninsulas up the coast from here. It was ever so in my imagination, ever such a part of my scheming and thinking about her that this should be her home, her ruin, her scattered dreams. I also thought how she could do better. She could do better with me.

She walked back into the centre of the room, her hair had fallen across her face; the strands of hair that should have been lovely crossed her tear-soaked cheeks; her eyes were blotchy and she looked like a maniac, sodden with bitterness.

'I'll show you she screamed you'll see for yourself you liar, you liar. Italian fathers are the worst of all. Shit abusers every last one of them; when they're not

slobbering at the confessional window or at the altar
every Sunday but wait until Wednesday when it gets
dark on the stairs and all that incense shit is off them;
then you'll see what they're like.'

She sat up, fumbled for the stash in her purse and
drew out a packet of cigarette papers. She smoothed
out a paper full, rolled it, double wrapped it, licked it
pinched the end and handed it to me.

I took it, looked at it and said, 'that will do me.'

She rolled one for herself, then arose and closed all the
dirty windows tight, clamped them firm at the latches
with brass screws. She dragged a blanket off the bed
and laid it against the crack in the door. She looked
around slowly then she looked at me. She smiled. A
sea change came over her features, but the eyes still
gave the game away.

'Are you sure you can take it old man,' she said. 'Everyone acts differently. Maybe you'll feel sad and start
to cry.'

'Don't worry about me.' I said.

She lit hers, held the match for mine.

'Inhale,' she said, 'then hold it, hold it until it hurts then let it out.'

'It reminds me of the big forest,' I said.

I inhaled. I held it a long time; then I let it out. She lay back against the divan and I did the same. Her feet dangled over the edge amongst the pile of tattered clothes.

'Sometimes it takes two,' she said.

We smoked them down until they burned our fingertips. Then I rolled two more. In the middle of the second it began to come, the floating, the wafting away on the breeze, the joy and triumph of my body over any ruin of time ; the extraordinary sense of power of those dark nights on the Amazon under cover of the trees and Maria Fidela , of Nancy and the blowing Chinese streets of the Barbary coast, all those coasts that drew me to the sea and away from the six sided clock out in the river from the Salisbury dock, places where I was happy to stay, even if Mary Jane did not want me at home; there was a world beyond that brown and silver river so wildly freshened by each new turbulent tide.

Rita was sitting at my feet, her hands on my knees, staring at me with those hungry eyes, tremendous eyes so large I could lose myself in them. She was dressed the same as I saw her the first time, the same clothes and the place was so desolate, I knew she had no others. The Bucko saw the sculpture of that young face under those eyes and through the bones of her cheeks; it was all written there, a face barely passed adolescence and a time she wouldn't see much longer. All written.

She lay back, the languor of the late afternoon upon her, the cynical passion, her ruined face, but I was gone beyond the room by then, floating in a land of bright moons and blinking stars. I was invincible even to my own poor life, my own poor people. I had never been that fellow with his grim happiness, his stage bravery. I had never been that Crazy Horse or buccaneer Bucko Johnny. I was somewhere else, deep in the warmth and rags of a tenement court building where all of us slept under coats and I gazed down on all of my poor family, on my brothers, my sister and on my poor dead Ma, as if from heaven.

An electric lamp stood on the table beside me, I picked it up and studied its filaments as if all the rivers in the world were leading to its one sad destination. As I looked it dropped to the floor. It broke into many pieces. She heard the noise, saw the smashed bulb and laughed.

'What's funny,' I said.

She laughed again and I got up crossed the room and took her in my arms. My whole body felt strong, and she panted at my crush and desire. I watched her stand and take off her clothes. I looked at her face, a child's face born out of obedience and fear, and I knew what was to become of her sooner or later. She crept into my arms, and I tried to sooth away her tears.

When it was all gone, all gone from me, the great heat, the dream of floating towards the bursting stars and the flesh returning to hold my blood in line with all its roaring channels, when the room returned, the dirty room, the sick building, the vacant meaningless ceiling, the weary wasted world of her life, I sat beside her as she lay on the divan and stared at the carpet. The Bucko stared too.

I saw the pieces of glass from the broken lamp and when I got up to walk across the room, I avoided them like a cat does. Too many lives had been shared in guilt and torn flesh; what was any blood of mine to do with that?

I left that apartment and began the long walk back to the Mission under the gaze of the astonished southern stars and the blue and black texture of the unfolding night. I could see my room and my cabin at Kwinana before me and all the peace I should have had with her but I also knew it was done.

I worked every hour those last three weeks and never saw a bunk ashore They were making me retire but time was all I had, and I was going to use it for that last big pay- off. When I came finally to the Mission, I asked around, but no one had seen her.

The next morning, I went out to Kwinana. She had been there looking for me, but she was not there now.

I went again to that sick diseased building, the place close to the water she called home. The black pock- marked features from another age still stood there, failing, old and tired, a dust filled shell. Her room was open, but she was not there either. All the clothes and rubbish were heaped into a pile in the centre of the floor looking as if they were ready to be fumigated burned or thrown. The Landlady said she'd left leaving the door open, just gone. Her mouth hung down and she looked at her rough hands then at her shoes, as if expecting to find something there, some clue or answer.

'I'm sorry,' she said.

Others said they had seen Rita aboard an Italian freighter berthed at the docks; that maybe she was trying to get home, to work her passage back across the ocean and they gave a shifty, mirthless laugh. Maybe that was why she was interested in my shining unblemished discharge book? They laughed again the bastards, hopeless Mission laughter.

I went to that dealing house she had taken me to; only days after she had told me to kiss her and laughed and cried and looked at me with those big sad eyes. I walked around the same corner and continued until I came to that same alley and that same doorway a couple of paces along surrounded by a broken brick wall and overflowing trash bins.

Now she was one of the people inside with faces that looked like ghosts. She saw me and started to scream. As I walked up to the mattress, she pulled up her knees and slipped into a crouched frightened position. She put her hands to her face as if she expected me to slap her or as if to hide herself completely from my sight. A couple of the guys looked over, but I was old and held no menace. I raised my hands, palms facing outwards. Another Joey came puffing out of a door in a tee shirt, the main man, the pimp; he was muscled and wore patent leather shoes.

'I've got money,' I said. 'I'm getting her out of here.'

She was still screaming; I shook her to keep her quiet. I passed over some notes and they let us go.

'See you soon,' the Boss said.

I could see him in those shiny shoes at lilac evening standing in the doorway of his users brothel, his feet tapping the pavement; he'd be announcing the merchandise to the passersby; a woman with creamy skin but covered in moles and another given to fantasies of the flesh and another with the whine and roar of a broken winch and some others from a foreign country and still another who forgets her name at every turn but inside them all there is only one woman. He isn't lying. Rita is every woman in that building and he is like every Pimp across the world, twenty years ago the Bucko would have battered him.

I bought food and made her eat; it was only milk and juice at first. She liked Grape juice because of its sweetness. I bought some clothes, just to get out of the rags she had been lying in with in that smoke filled room where they all believed they were angels.

Bit by bit I got her through.

She came to stay out at Kwinana. She didn't seem to worry about the nearly forty years between us. She even seemed to like the fresh air and the good drink we'd have when I came home.

'It's quiet here,' she said 'but I can always hear something.'

'It's the sea,' I said. 'Just like opening and closing your front door.' She nodded quietly.

There were no drugs in my cabin, but she didn't seem to mind that either. I could forget the in between times when I was away, or she was downtown. We had some good times, close times, in those months.

Then I went on a small jag, a last- minute cover job, just around the Bight to Albany; I'd left her with Michael Curran and his brother Thomas. They had a house by the cove. When I came back three days later, they told me she'd gone.

'Gone, gone where,' I said, 'You were supposed to be

looking out for her.'

Michael looked at the ground.

'We had a party, 'he said.

He looked at his brother, Tommy's lower lip was still wet, and he was trembling.

'She was drinking and smoking and going crazy,' he said.

I knew there was more.

'Some party,' I said.

I saw again those figures from the dead house; dead to the sunlight and the wind that had brought them here from across the sea to this blazing, bright land so full of dreams.

'We tried to calm her, but she just screamed some more.' Michael said.

'She said she needed the water to get clean.'

'You fools, 'I said but I knew by their faces they knew

they had fucked up so I didn't say too much.

I looked around for Rita for the next few days but somehow I knew the Ocean had her; that business with the Italian freighter was just the make believe; just a glimpse of the water and people moving across it would be enough, the waves to carry her, the winds to soothe her, the bright dazzling blue to console her and let her wheel away on those once strong arms, swimmers arms, her father had brought with him from Calabria that sometimes also held her down, where she knew the pattern of cracks on the ceiling better than any other fact in her life; where her Mama didn't know any of it. My old man had also swum away his visions back to Cork but it is no way to return with your body full of water and your face bloated like a swollen doll.

'Don't talk to me of Italian Fathers,' she had screamed.

There was no solitude, no escape. I heard about her jumping from the furthest fishing pier, no sympathy, no relief. I lay down and cried and even the calmness of Maria Fidela who was always the image at the head of my own bunk when I rustled the pillow in loneliness or desperation was no consolation to the Bucko now.

Rita seemed so far away, and I could not bring her back not even her image. I felt myself slowly filling with sadness and shame; you fool, why did you go away; you had enough money you should have stayed and helped her you stupid old man; you did what you pleased with her and now she's gone. You should have helped her, done more.

All through the nights she mangled my sleep. I saw her hair weaving out as she went under; saw it like I had seen it with my Da George Alexander, but the voices kept singing, you didn't help her, you didn't keep her safe, what use your big plans now? I was full of shame and guilt. I kept searching for her body to keep from going crazy. That's when the tourists found me; I didn't find them. They were out beyond the piers, out of their depth just where the tidal marker had received Rita's body. She was the one who I was looking for, not them, the fools.

There was nothing to say, the haze on the horizon, the sea a sheet of pearl and filtered over it a diffuse yellow, small figures played against the vast shore and the rocks with the sky over their shoulders; all the complex wires of life stripped out and I could see the structure, the pure simplicity of living but Rita was no longer part of it and instead I had another case of the nearly submerged and drowned on my hands. What else could I do?

In, 'Dangerous waters' the papers said. They gave my occupation as 'Boatman,' which they said is all what ex seafarers are called when they leave the sea, the huers. First a fisherman and then a boatman! Where did they get these terms from? Retire, shellbacks never retire. That hero business felt as if it had been manufactured on the press room floor, brought out of a museum of old newspaper stories, strap headlines that didn't quite fit but would do anyway for the suckers.

I had no need to ask myself why? The shame of being with her and letting her die; the shame for all those poor fuckers killed and maimed in the war; the war I had refused. The shame of being with such a young woman, of being with Rita; it wasn't any excuse but it could have been? How I loved those mad eyes, how beautiful she was, I felt so bad, I had failed her. I thought she had not changed because I did not do enough.

The papers said I was fishing but I knew what I was doing. No body had yet been found. Those tourists just happened to be lucky. There was no drama. But the story went straight to the press and in these tough years, the papers wanted any good story they could get. The editors loved it; they sold it big. I hated it. It rubbed salt into my shame. They gave less than two lines to Rita Acello.

'Young woman goes missing off fishing pier; parents distraught.'

In the Amazon, the traders used to tell a story, 'let us say you are with your lover, let's say she loves you, let's say that she wants to take control of your body through persuasion or violence when you take the medicine of the leaves, let's say she is blowing warm air over your left ear, the most sensitive one, the one she knows makes you crazy. Let's say you could stop her if you wanted, if you really wanted, but you let her carry on, be tickled, enjoy your time, keep your trap shut. What will be will be. You will never know when death comes.' I thought of that trader with his Catholic insurance policy and the hard eyes of the steel rimmed Jesuit priest.

'Of course, my son, special measures call for special offerings on the part of the Penitent.'

Rita knew. I had been looking for here ever since, but it was like looking into a mirror. Australia was no different from the Amazon except it had the Oceans and the wind and she was far from the desert of southern Italy, but she made her choice between the sands and the rolling blue. I had looked for her a million times in the months that followed but she belonged to the big sea now.

I sold the Kwinana cabin and gave the money to the Mission. They'd looked after me long enough. After my supposed 'heroics' of saving the tourists from a watery death there were plenty of free drinks for me down there. I bathed my feet in false sentiment hoping for relief but I knew there was none to come for my shame. In my own mind it was a sign. Rita provided me with that sign just as surely as those Indians of the forest accepted with good grace their last voyage. I did not need a blackened tenement, the Celtic Sea nor a murderer's knife to remind me of the deaths that had studded my life like stars against a cruel sky, of little Amelia, my old man or poor Francis James. I had a last swallow with a couple of old mates and told them I was going Bush and not to expect me back. My head was clear, the Bucko had done his time.

They laughed.

'You'll see your arse,' they said.

Eight

I walked to the Wellington Street station next morning and took a bus from Freo to Perth and from there onto the national route in the direction of the Exmouth peninsula. From Carnarvon I hailed an old truck away from the peeling red paint of the bus sheds at the double crossroads and travelled with it to the grass lit fringes of the Little Sandy desert.

When I jumped down from that bus, the Bucko knew what he was doing; it's nearly 800 miles up the coast towards the peninsula but I wasn't going that far. You can get to the desert before that, and you don't need to take the Canning Stock Route either.

The Canning dock in Liverpool was named after a city politician of the early part of the 19th Century who later became leader of the Conservative Party and made prime minister post the Napoleonic wars. I'd sailed from that dock many a time. His Uncles had made big money out of the slave trade and after that the European conflagrations. His family might have started in Ireland, like mine but he soon became a big man over here, famous for the transportations and penal colonies that riddled this land. It wouldn't take you too much to work out what the Stock stood for?

Back in Liverpool the City Burghers did what they do the world over, hung his name high over the balustrades and named one of the oldest docks after him and later a desert highway here in the Antipodes. Bully for them says the Bucko; what else would they entitle him with, maybe *The Canning Middle Passage* or perhaps the *Canning Goree Piazza* named after that blasted stretch of Guinea basalt where they embarked the poor souls onto ships for the Americas. Those dignitaries were all rapists of one kind or another. I wonder what names they gave in San Francisco to places where they razed the Chinese from their waterfront homes?

On the journey we passed the wreck of the rusted red town of Cervantes. No great books were written where I was going, neither windmills nor horses but let nobody tell you that seamen don't read. You got sneak views of the water peeking out through the green country as the old green and gold bus scrambled North onto the Indian Ocean Road. Alongside the coast, brown tilled acres rapidly turned to yellow bush before you got far out of that town, then a flash of blue again, shot with grey, the last I would see of the Ocean except in my dreams.

Carnarvon lies in a fold of earth where the coast meets the outback and begins to skirt the tracks of the Little Sandy. It was good to leave behind the rows of pitted houses and see the land change from farmland and small brown hills to the more arid ochre colour of the scrub. Wild goats dotted the empty landscape.

We approached the town through garden orchards and stopped at a store with an iron roof called Morel's. I bought some dried fruit. Morel had a son who had sailed with me and gave me tobacco on the side and wanted to give me wine, but I refused it. When the bus continued on its way to the peninsula, I stepped out into the dust and padded to the crossroads.

The country all around is flat and vast as if it was always reminding you of the desert beyond. Termite mounds rise to greet you like tiny hills. There are thousands of them, ridge after ridge and the air blows through them in a soft resonant blue like a bellows and raises the hot sinewy dust and only settles with the still, cold nights and low, bright moons.

The mounds are strung like beads, in huge numbers all along the Minilya road. I took a last look at where I thought the sea should be across those thousands of miles and tried to imagine that other place beneath its canopy of trees with the black river running through it and her shining black hair and the memories it brought of her odour and leaves, love and rain. I couldn't.

Behind a screen of tamarisks was an old unpainted tin bungalow, grey growing over into rust what had once been a green sheet, with a cracked brick chimney growing up the middle. This was my mate Christy Cain's cabin. He was residing at the Mission down in Freo and recovering from the terrors of drink.

The Mission looked after us seafarers. It bossed us about as if we possessed no thoughts of our own on dry land and gave us fiery sermons on the perils of the juice, but it was kind in its own ways. The women who volunteered there were servants of the local church or were married to the Pastor and generally worked hard at redeeming lost souls. They were there to help, and they did but the women we liked were generally unknown to them. The likes of Rita Acello they tried to shoo away; the shadows of their clean print dresses blowing in the wind.

I stayed a day or more in Christy's broken cabin to get my bearings and kept my last tobacco from Morels and prepared myself for the journey. I crossed within site of the Carnarvon mountains and then struck out for the interior then after a period of three hours, hitched down another old and rusty roustabout truck. The engine belched and forged right and headed east along a dusty road that ran next to a rocky incline. The road rose and fell through a thicket of grey leaves and there were pale hawks perched on the fence posts of a landing line. Away over to the East there was an outcrop of weathered red sandstone with a range of pinnacles some about twenty foot high. I knew it had to be an Aboriginal site where they had sat and dreamed of footsteps tracing ancestral spirits over each earthly print of this blasted golden land.

I was heading towards it through the spinifex and the mulgara scrub. Ghost gum trees watched me go by. After what seemed like hours of bumping around the Roustabouts dropped me down where I asked.

One of them said, 'this is a rough country Bud, good luck.'

He could see the Bucko was old. No one asked where I was going. Perhaps they knew. Maybe that was a death truck I could see scuttling off in a cloud of blue smoke. Around mid- afternoon I crossed a creek with river red reeds growing in its bed, I picked my way over waterworn boulders and pools of yellow stagnant liquid where the mosquitoes had mixed with water in a slurry of broken wings and dead leaves across the black surface. The country further east was grey and treeless and cloud shadows moved across it, no cattle, no fences no wind pumps. I knew I was nearly there by the absence of flies.

I passed a withered gum, a cloud of black cockatoos shot out, squawking, their cries like doors on rusty hinges. They settled up ahead to where I was heading to the sand, the occasional red flash shot beneath their wings as they opened and closed them, settled then scattered again, always fighting and squawking as if for life itself.

The yellow limestone grew fierce under the sun. Coloured streaks of mineral sediment shone against the red sand and black rock. It was like watching an entire army that had been turned to stone while standing guard over the water and watching for invaders; a reminder of how we watched for narks in Ireland before my trial nearly forty years ago or how these native peoples studied European explorers and the settlers who arrived in ships from the West and wondered who they were and what they wanted? More than forty years, the difference between me and Rita Acello.

'Are you my rich sailor,' I hear her ask me and she demands I kiss her with the bums from the mission surly laughter ringing in my ears

I was nearly home now, beyond the outcrops and salt rock; to sit straight backed at my place, my oasis, my tree. Nowhere has truth so short a life as in these deserts of the West, the Vicky, the Gibson and the Little Sandy. It is a constant wonder to me that when something has happened five minutes before, its source of truth has vanished just like the squabbling cocka-toos, camouflaged, embellished, disfigured, squashed, annihilated by imagination, shame, or fear. Gone for-ever. Five minutes before all life had existed to that one single point now departed, like seeing the colour of time being painted each new minute.

In this territory any story soon vanishes. Rita was from the deserts and wide grasslands, and she went to the Ocean. The Bucko is from an Ocean town with a river as its main high street and I am going now to the desert. So it is, so it is meant to be. Nowhere except here in these places is history dismantled so quickly, with no backward glance. What is not held within you is not worth knowing.

I had worked with a thousand seamen down these coasts who had all known the power of Shipping Companies, their federations, trusts and family dynasties. We knew where we had come from in the famine parishes and those who wished to keep us there but without our song; nothing. Even now, even though you could not see it, you could feel that wind hard off the bay, a roll of cloud on the edge of the sea and the green and white waves rolling to meet the icebergs so far down to the South.

I am grateful for those impenetrable jumbles of people who looked after me, not with the insistent regret of the old who sit on benches and watch the young go by with disgust or feast with a blind loyalty on the days made golden by laughter or song, the warmth of fire. The Bucko walks amongst them now like an outsider but their dancing shadows rise before me as a young man and even in those crowded Courts; those dark musty rooms with all of us sleeping under overcoats, there are days and times indeed when desire for that age is deep within me. When you dream is when you live; is that why the sky is always blue? Do these matters belong to God? I was always a Catholic.

Forever present to see again my mother and father and brothers, the brothers who are dead before me,

Francis James and George, and others who are living, William Patrick and Henry; so easy to love them all when so many beds have been offered that you sometimes wonder on what side of the blanket you yourself have been born. My sister Mary Agnes and poor dead Amelia and you could add to their number Mary Jane Ross and lovely Rita Acello. The Bucko well remembers the black lustre of her eyes.

'He has the money,' I hear her say to the peddler, the pimp, the runner of women from that diseased house with its black pock marked walls.

I remember the wild depth of her, the jolt in my stomach, old as I am, the days I had first known her and made her laugh. If I hadn't of taken that jag to Albany, if I hadn't left her with the Currans. I wanted to help her, to get her away from those sick houses, those raggedy curtained traps, away from those smoke and death rooms, I wanted her to get away, if she could only get away with me but the sea has her now and it is useless.

An old song they used to sing rises up inside me, an old song that kills me with its sentiment. I used to cry when they sang it in all the salt bars across the waterfront.

'She blew smoke across my tears, shared jokes in the dust, then she disappears, I never knew her trail, a blanket for our love, whose passage lights and fails, what brought her here, in the lilac dusk, a woman once so clear, ice blue on the rails, a dancer till she's bust, absorbed in all her days, no one could get near, a spark never dull, she swallowed all my fears, they haunt me like I failed, I did what I could, rolled smoke in yellow paper, stored away the years, the odour of her musk, across the bar ten beers, did I betray her trust?'

'We'll take another one Bucko there is always tomorrow,' I hear George's voice come singing off the Manhattan piers.

Sick of it all , I try to face the ordeal of seeking forgiveness, but from whom, from God, from Christ from the Communion of the Holy Spirit? These are fairy tales from the myths I once believed in. But Our Holy Mother proclaims, this is the sea and the sea is eternal, this is the sea and I believe it is real and I turn from the sea and everywhere I look there is land. I walk on and on and still the land goes stretching away but I know there is still the sea, the prayer is within me.

'You are nothing and I might once have been something,' says Nancy in all the blowing blue of San

Francisco, the green jade scarf she always wore folded neatly beside her on the chair of the café' where we ate. She stares at me across the table. We take a drink.

And I ask her where is the sea, where is the sea that Rita Acello perished on and she answers, 'the sea is back there, it will always be back there.' It might be a myth for my memory, but it will always stay within me. The sea is real. I was born on its shore. I bathed in its waters. It gave me food and it gave me peace and its distance fed my dreams.

The Bucko smiles. I am here in this soulless desert and far from its bounty, but the salt of the sea is in my blood and there maybe ten thousands roads over the land but they will not confuse me. I shall return to my homeland if only in spirit, that is why the desert has chosen me now to keep the sea alive forever within me. I shall be forgiven for that, for Nancy and Maria Fidela and for poor Rita Acello and for all my tattered and lost commandments.

'I don't want you to see my ribbons Johnny,' Mary Jane moves in the yellow sourball light of a Liverpool summer above the North docks, the detritus of the slum pub strewn all around us, men hanging off the brown tables, men falling down at the bar beneath the kegs and barrels ; the places we visit and the crowded parishes we inhabit; all around us and people are dancing with their poor misbegotten possessions and souls you can see enjoying themselves all down Scotland Road on a Saturday night.

Our Lady of the hopeless hope please help me. People are good here, people are kind, people are good everywhere, everyone gets frightened and sometimes lost but they don't panic, they are brave people, they are a long way from their original homes here in the great and golden land but they have brought their bravery with them. They are tough, they aren't afraid of anything. They have crossed the Oceans to be here, the Bucko is with them in spirit. Dear God, please help me.

'Did you never want to be a father yourself Johnny,' someone once asks me?

I tell them I am still reliving my first trips to sea in those cold and wet summers of 1880-1881 fifty years ago. These are my children.

A poet once said, 'we spend the first third of our lives in bright darkness and the second two thirds trying to recover it.' That made sense to me.

I didn't have children; I didn't want children. You can't lead this life if you have kids, useless if you have a family with you. I could not have led them through the dance of my times. Those present are enough for anyone where I come from; Bucko Johnny Brown born in a poor parish and baptised on Scotland Road; family enough on that long ribbony mass packed against the water and polished as the brass nails of the crucifix, with names in golden letters etched on wooden boards and stones in graveyards all along the river. Did my Old Man really see the lights of Cork twinkling across the Celtic Sea before his big swim?

The living have their own cross. Their prayers are enough for me. Those still alive will have them printed against their very being. My mother's last words for our Francis James, 'Oh Sweet Heart of Jesus, Guide his Soul' so sadly cut down on the last day of Passchendaele and my tears for our George on that murderous quayside of Bahia Blanca.

The Bucko loved him. He was my closest brother both in age and spirit. I loved Mary Jane his wife but she found a new husband and the son was taken in with her, thank god. But it took five years of them grinding it out, a widow living with her sister's husband and family within a blackened tenement to know the difference between what I knew already in my heart.

Crazy Horse arranged for his squaw to be looked after. He knew what he was doing that feller, he knew he wouldn't come out of that Fort Robinson alive. It hadn't been that bad even if I'd got it wrong with Mary Jane. She was looked after.

It is finished now with the middens, court houses, tenements and cellars that produced me. I danced with those angels over so many years and discovered looking down at my body that testament to be my witness in the corpus that time has beaten. Time is passing through me now, time as the thief, the mugger; time for our blessed mother Caroline Brown (1834 -1919) who prayed for us all, the dead souls and living and who has now arrived back to the stations of her days. Liverpool's a laugh but it is not always a happy place.

My back is rigid and straight; I have waited for this freezing darkness. It has been long in coming; George on a Friday night, Francis James on a Saturday morning and me tonight on one slow Sunday, a perfect trilogy. We go in turn if not in order. My poor dear Rita. I throw my battered journal to the wind in honour of your name; like I threw my English discharge book to the Ocean; sand for me, water for you, within our troubled communion.

The last great voyage; I feel the rush of air from the desert as if it were from my own lungs the great hot breath of an unknown land that has become mine; the sudden stirrings like the final bleat of a sacrificial lamb; no matter that I was Baptised at Saint Anthony's, George at Holy Cross, Francis at Saint Alexanders, Billy at Saint James – and Henry God knows where but all our great joys are remembered along the river, deep within its waters, along its sandy shore. I wonder where I will wake tomorrow like my father who must have known, despite his great fever that this was his last striking out for home, the surging waves, the lights, the eternal darkness; Bucko you have tried to live.

I can smell the sea even from here, or the thought of the sea that would always make me live even in this desert but this place has claimed me now just as the waters claimed Rita Acello. I take the Old Man's rosary from my pocket and hold the beads; so hail then and farewell and bless myself before this broken altar, I am going home, a *despedida*.

THE PENTHSILEA

A sailing ship built with an iron hull in 1867. George Wailey, John Brown's father joined her in 1871 as a seaman on deck when he was 38 years old. You can see her berthed at Brisbane during the great flood of 1873 which swamped the City after huge tides in the South Pacific had swollen the fifty mile length of the river. She had made the voyage from Liverpool to the Australian Coast in 44 days.

Nine

George Alexander Wailey 1832 -1887
Aussie, Liverpool, Cork.
(Derived from a story by George Garrett, 1934)

As she comes away from the heat of Africa and the bulge of Old Calabar, the *Roquelle* encounters an Atlantic Storm. A steam schooner with three sails, two masts and a boiler she belches noxious thick bl ack smoke across the Atlantic. A new ship only three years old in 1887 and built on the Clyde for the Elder Dempster Company on the Liverpool West Africa run, she is finishing her sixth voyage and is now proceeding home from Dakar when she encounters terrible weather south of the Bay of Biscay.

None of these threats of the rising storm, can quieten any of the half-a-dozen sailors arguing noisily on this side of the poky, dismal forecastle. And almost in pitch darkness too, for no light enters through the tightly screwed iron lids that blind the three small portholes. The singing double oil-lamps are lit, throwing a yellow glimmer on the men's bobbing faces like figures from an oil painting around a card table as their voices rise higher and louder, unmindful of George Alexander

Wailey and his torment and agitated detachment as he lies sick in a low bunk. Even Big Conlan in his excitement has forgotten him, his old watchmate.

There is no separate place for him to lie, and nowhere else for the men to sit, so he can't escape their noisy din as their faces twist in anger and confusion. They are interrupted by the ringing of seven o'clock on deck, and the surprise entry of young long-fingered Mahoney a junior ordinary seaman, who comes with a wince on his face, hurting with his damaged left hand but bursting with information. through the open companionway.

Straightaway he gains the men's attention with startling news of the wild black cat; he swears sprung at him a few minutes previously off a coil of rope by the 'Rosie' on the after end Well deck. When asked to describe it, he continues with a rapid stream of details:

'It's nearly as big as a Newfoundland dog; has a rough coat like a porcupine and two great yellow eyes like oil lamps.'

'Has it come for me, thank God? 'George inquires in a grossly morbid tone.

'Ah,' Big Conlan butts in sarcastically, I suppose it has the Sandhills of Cork harbour tattooed on its tail.'

During this uproar, George twists restlessly in the bunk. Sweat drenches his vest. Apart from himself and Conlan the remainder of the men are apparently convinced that Mahoney is telling the truth. A couple of them, though not having actually seen the thing, swear they have heard its hideous wailing. In their opinion its presence abroad is a warning of some kind of trouble. Across the forecastle in their dark corner you can hear the stokers murmur the same and the atmosphere gradually quietens down to a low sulfurous pessimism.

As Mahoney leaves the forecastle, Duffy a tall man, turns a grave face to the others:

'I think,' he says 'I honestly think, that this auld Hooker's cursed. That cat's a sure sign of something; believe me.'

The sick man stirs uneasily in his bunk; his feverish condition aroused by the quarrelsome group around him.

'Jesus Christ,' he mumbles to himself, 'such crazy foolish twaddle; what awful rubbish from grown-up men.

Men! They're more like a drivelling collection of big, soft children. And just as ignorant, too. Yapping about these silly signs! You haven't enough brains to recognize real fights. What we need is change from all this.'

He gazes in despair at the ever-flowing stream of salt water that trickles down the bulkhead knowing eventually it would soon swell the pool under the bunk. As if there wasn't enough sniffy dampness to contend with from the dripping leakages above his head! Nothing would happen unless they all got together to change these lousy conditions instead of worrying about black cats or whistling down the wind and other superstitious nonsense.

Worst of all are the torturing noises that never seem to stop. The long continuous banging of the anchor chains in the chute by his elbow reminds him of jails in the 'States where drag-shackles are part of the prisoners' punishment. A jail, he reflects. No, not as good as a jail! on these hookers, even the new ones. In a jail, a really sick man can obtain medical attention, be put under the care of a qualified doctor, and sent to hospital if necessary. But here, in this squalid dump of a stinking forecastle there is no advantages of that kind, no decent accommodation for a man in his predicament.

Instead, everything adds to his discomfort. The pitching movement of the ship keeps constantly jerking a persecuted body from side to side of the low cramping wood. Grating on his nerves too, is the irregular slamming of unfastened locker doors as they swing open and shut with a bang. He stares agonizingly in their direction. What we need is better conditions, but no one is going to give them us unless we stick together. Without a scrap against the shipowners there'll be no gains. He stretches his aching limbs for relief. One vexing thought follows another like a carriage of wagons behind a dock engine.

'What a dreadful hellhole to be in,' he says to himself. 'To think that a man can't get a simple bottle of medicine no matter how badly he needs it; it's against the rules! Blast that 'midship gang and their bloody rules! Making a man wait until the turn of daylight, their time at the Dispensary and for what? Pills! That was all they could think about. Just pills! Pills!! Pills!!! Poultices! Pox medicines! And their detestable black draught! Ugh! The taste of it. Ugh! What a horrible concoction to bring anybody; bloody griping purgatives for a man suffering and burning wretched in every bone of his body.'

He rolls over on to his side, but unable to settle in that position he twists onto his front. The effects of the malarial infection are there for all to see along his dripping frame.

'Oh, I wish I was home and out of this. What's the use of having five sons if not one of them can help their old man now? My Caro could fix me up right away, and with less ceremony. She would guess the trouble in half-a-tick and know exactly what to do. A nurse in the Southern hospital before she marries me in that hot July a quarter of a century ago.'

'Dear oh dear, he struggles to remember the year but know it to be in the early 'Sixties in Saint Peter's on Seel Street just before they built the Lady chapel. The same time we moved to the North end with our Mary Agness and our John before the rest of the kids born in Kirkdale, then back to our dark tenements after the christenings that we fill along the dock road like rats in their holes, like priests walking their famine parishes, but anything better than this. Oh, Jesus even in the dismal blackness it would be better than on this old coffin box.'

He turns and looks at the porthole anxiously, the stream continues and he thinks My god when will it ever end ? We need a union; a union for everyone who has ever landed at the Clarence dock or sailed from the Pier head. His head tosses back and forth with the pitch of the ship, and he dreams of the shining bright Sandhills of Cobh where he was born and raised.

Seven bells ring out along the deck. Immediately afterwards, young Mahoney steps back, quieter this time into the forecastle, carrying with his good hand a couple of Dixies containing a frugal refreshment for two men.

'Twenty minutes past seven,' he announces in a cautious undertone to the watch, and noiselessly lays the food on the narrow table. He takes a sly peep at George Alexander whose eyes are shut, and then whispers close into Conlan's ear:

'I've been told not to call him. Bennett has offered to stay on deck and work on for two hours. He says you would get one of the others to relieve him by then.'

Conlan puts a hushing finger to his lips for he quickly anticipates the rest of Mahoney's message. Duffy is near at hand and overhearing what has been said, is also anxious to do his share. Ordinarily, he was not due to go on duty until next watch at twelve. Under the present circumstances however, he is willing to start two hours earlier and whispers so to Conlan who nods in agreement.

'It's the best plan Joe,' he says, 'letting him lie for a watch or two. It will give him a good chance of pulling round. The rest of us can work the job between us somehow.'

As he says this George Alexander twists in his bunk and opens his eyes. He gazes beyond the now quietly conversing men seated near and to the dark corner where the half-naked Conlan is changing into his deck gear.

Duffy is packing his clay pipe with tobacco. Inside himself, the inner core of George Alexander Wailey feels an intense bitterness towards these two men. So, they think he has not been listening! He has heard every word said. That blasted Dispensary midships; they make an exception for the kid with his bad hand but not for him. Dear Jesus, he is burning up and all these two have been discussing is him and his sickness, and what they intend to do.

THE CITY OF RICHMOND

Originally an Inman Line ship that switched to the American Line. As a liner she was chiefly engaged in the emigrant trade between Liverpool, New York, Baltimore and Newport News. George joined her in 1875 when thousands of Liverpool seamen were making the transition from sail to steam.

His shoulders sink. He wearily drags his body into a sitting position, and half leans out of the side of his bunk. His eyes feel as hot as his body and seem unusually wide even to himself. His face is as pinched as a pick and burns like a furnace around the small tight spots beneath his cheekbones. He glares disdainfully at those about him, but particularly at Conlan and Duffy.

His sudden emergence has made all the men uncomfortable, tongue-tied, and fidgety. One of them tries to hide his embarrassment in a clumsy attempt to fasten the locker doors. He can feel Conlan's eyes upon his drenched back.

Conlan keeps up this observation for a few seconds and then he looks round the forecastle again. He watches George stretch his body farther out of the bunk to put his feet onto the deck; fearing he might fall he crosses over to him and inquires in a kindly apprehensive tone:

'Do you need anything, George?'

'Me, the sick man?' He stares quizzically before waiting to reply:

'Who?' 'Me? Me want anything from youse. No. I don't

want anything.' And he curtly waves him aside.

'Mind out will yer! Get out of the way.'

Lifting his wobbly legs, he struggles into his working pants as all the other men sit slyly watching him. After buckling the waist belt tight, he stares accusingly from Conlan to the rest in turn and blurts out between heavy breaths:

'What's the matter with all of you? Eh? Sitting there like a crowd of dummies! A rake of crows. You're not bawling the place down now, are you? Raving about your bloody champions and your black cats. Its babies' rattles you ought to have, all of youse. Something for you to play with! Yes, that's what you want; something to amuse you.'

Inwardly he steams; why did Conlan go to see Caroline Wailey his wife. Did he have something to say about his brother, the brother that had been bothering her from the old days?

He pokes his chest assertively as he turns on Conlan again. 'I suppose you thought I wouldn't go abroad on this watch?' he says. 'Well, I am going on deck.' He coughs to clear his throat. 'I'm more than thirty years at this sea-game, savvy! Nobody ever did a watch for me yet. And' he adds in a hoarse shout, 'they're not starting now.'

As he bends over to grope on the floor for his boots, he suddenly lifts his head in a pointed challenge to all around.

'Do you think I'll be beholden to any of youse: you sodden gaggle of Board of Traders?'

Conlan ignores the deliberate insult and tries again in a gently persuasive tone to change George Alexander's obstinate intention.

'Get back into your bunk for your own benefit,' he entreats.

'You're not fit, George and you know it. Last night you staggered around like a drunken man.'

He carefully restrains from hinting that the extra exertion has meant him having to do most of that other man's work as well as his own. In an earnest intimate approach, he sits down on the form alongside his shipmate whose trembling fingers are taking an age to knot a bootlace.

'George,' he pleads, 'What's the use of carrying on this way when you know you're unfit, come on, there's a good lad. Get back into your bunk. You're not right to go up there!'

The sick man, wipes his brow, straightens up, edges away from Conlan and barks jerkily in return: 'Not fit? Who's not fit? What are ye talking about? The deck was laid out all watch, wasn't it? The wheel honed, the mates served; all on the button, the hatches checked, the red lead set out for the day men, the lamplighter stores gauged.'

'Treating me like a first tripper!' he turns upon all of them once more and snaps his fingers. 'Ye can't teach me about the deck, none of yer,' I was sailing AB before most of you hit the sunlight. 'No, not that much eh! Thought I wouldn't go up on top, eh? Huh!' Thought I couldn't make it?'

Conlan patiently controls his anger and decides to yield.

'Just as you like, Buddy,' he says indulgently. 'Please yourself,' and carries on rolling a cigarette. The quarrel has robbed both himself and George Alexander of an appetite; the Dixies containing their dinner lay untouched. *Bothering her indeed and he sends his brother to explain.*

One solitary bell strikes on deck: a quarter to eight. Instantly the two men jump to their feet, button their dungaree jackets and stride huffily apart out of the forecastle on to the forward deck, taking but a cursory glance up at the bridge where an officer, his sextant cocked, is measuring the arc of the night and the vessel's passage from the Bay to the Celtic Sea. George Alexander holds his head erect and shows no signs of lagging even in the big wind.

Pride gingers his gait and keeps him within a short distance of Conlan. The angry words forbade one friendly utterance as they hurry together along the open rails, nimbly dodging the spray and sprinkling spindrift that showers around them. Soon they enter an opening, aft of the saloon and by way of a long closed-in alleyway to reach the fiddley door, where the tall paint-peeled funnel rises high above their heads There is a moon jerking between ragged black clouds beside the lamplighter's store. The sea is still wild.

On the narrow cased-in grating below them they sit a few feet apart, glancing resentfully at each other while waiting for the watch bell to strike. In the close heat next to the stack their bodies soon warm to a sticky sweat. Below them come mixed clouds of rising smoke, gaseous fumes, and hissing steam that irritates their lungs and compels them both to hawk and spit. Thank God they did not have to go down to that hell pit.

On reaching the bulkhead Conlan strides briskly to the shelving and busies himself around the three huge racks of tools with his customary bustle and proficiency. Bennett, who has come down from the wheelhouse and has volunteered to do the extra hours', stands gaping as he watches them come up onto the deck plates then catching Conlan's significant glance, understands and without any further comment trudges to the long ladder leading down to his berth below.

Left to themselves the other two begin their tasks together as the circumstances demand. Not a single word passes between them. Selecting the necessary tools, long hoes, and chipping bars, they tie them down in convenient rows by that section of the deck marked for the removal of barnacles and tar on the morning watch. No storm was going to change that.

Conlan walks to the centre of the deck beneath the second mast and looks at the steam gauge and whether they would have to make sail; but even with this wind, there is no signal from the bridge. While taking a breather he casts a discreet wary eye on his watch mate sitting almost doubled up at the valve box at the base of the mast.

Just getting to the deck with the tools has left George Alexander in utter exhaustion; he flops helplessly against the battened sail chest that sits next to the valves. The mast rises above him with its yellow crow's head lantern. A long swig of water from the drinking can does not improve his condition. His bulging red-and streaky eyes stare at the crackling sparks coming from the funnel. The fires from below are burning like hell but so is he!!! With an effort he bends over, unties his deck boots, drags them off, and pours from them a stream of accumulated sweat that has run down off his body and legs.

Conlan reaches for his dungaree jacket and holds it out for him, but he would have none of it. His straying hands rub feverishly against his forehead and his throat, and an occasional spasm shudders the base of his neck. Something was catching at his breath. 'Phew!' he gasps. 'The heat! Phew!! Oh, suffering' Jeez. It's terrible. It's terrible.' Conlan thought in truth the summer night was still cool for that time of year but how can you tell that to a man suffering the deliriums of a malarial fever.

George Alexander staggers off the box and reaching for the sail stores flops down once more. His body is in torment, his mind too. If he could only manage to last out the remainder of the four hours, just to finish his time!

He began to moan and grunt to himself. 'Oh,' he says. 'Oh, I must have some air, the air you can only attain on the Well deck.' Rising unsteadily to his feet, he gropes in front of him and stumbles instinctively in the direction of the long ladder beyond the after hatches that lead away to the stern.

Conlan, on alert, promptly hurries across, and seizes his arm: 'Hey! Come back here! Where do you think you're off to?' he demands.

George Alexander struggles to pull his arms free as he shows traces of his old belligerence.

'Let go of me,' he says. 'Go on! Hands off!'

Conlan tightens his powerful grip: 'Where Are You Going?'

'Down to the Well deck for a cooler: anything else you'd like to know?'

Conlan stares hard at him. He is losing patience, and raises his voice:

'I've already said don't go down there.'

'I'll put it nicely,' George says, 'now fuck off.'

George can see he wants to knock him down, but he's heard these Cogger's before. There's no limits to the insults he'll take because he's bigger and younger. Guilt will trip him up; next he'll be saying in the past few days he's done the work for two men and will have taken more insults from you that any man on earth should have to take but he still won't strike you down, it's the guilt thing.

He'll reason to himself, what's the use of hitting a man who is sick and bad-tempered; only a waste of breath to argue with him. But you George Alexander knows what it is to act like a man. You haven't been a packet rat for twenty years before sailing to this damn infected coast.

George hears Conlan sigh as he stands there, undecided what to do next, then glancing in alarm as a Mate's shadow appears on the bridge he dashes back to where his tools lay and starts to hoist them amidships.

His sudden turn causes the other man to topple forward. Clutching anxiously on the handrail ladder, George slowly intones *one, two, three* and then after several slithering attempts, succeeds in firmly placing his lagging feet on the mid rung and to shift his body around, his arms hug the bars at a level with his shoulders. He lowers his eyes to the sea, and slowly begins to descend.

The cold draught catches at his face. Ah, it's so refreshing. He can already feel the wonderful difference. His starved body craves for more; lots more of this cool sweet stuff; as much of it as possible. It makes him feel a little better, though the feet will not act as he wants them to.

At the bottom he crouches on his hands and knees and stares ahead as if hypnotized; then begins crawling along the lower deck parallel with the sea. This indeed is a godsend! Oh, and the wind; that brushes you gently as gently as a Carter with his horse! What a relief it means to his overheated body, his feverish mind. He must have more! He holds his mouth wide open as the wind rips across the ocean, to swallow that rush of oxygen; to gorge it into his throat and stomach; to enjoy its refreshing coolness right through your system. Ah heaven.

Out there is the water! Out there an unlimited quantity of everything; light, airy and cool refreshment so necessary to your great thirst. He is so parched, hellish parched; not on the lips alone, but all of him, in every pore that runs through his body.

'A plunge in the ocean that would be the thing.'

His mouth echoes the thought over and over to himself. One good plunge then back to the ship! He'd show these so-called sailors how to stream her.

A big sea is coming in. He hears its approach and sees its gathering momentum. 'Boom!' it goes as it strikes the midships. That will shake them.

'Boom' he laughs, 'shake them fuckers up, glass backs and so-called medicine men.'

In sheer delight he watches the deluge of water pour aboard, flow along the alleyway and down the gunnels. It laps at his sockless ankles.

'God! That was a beauty.' He feels invigorated.

Very soon he'll be out there and splashing up to the neck. Aye, only a couple of yards more to go, then he would be right in the heart of the ocean's caress. But how? That was a question. How? The bulkhead is a bit too high.

You must look for some place lower. Maybe worm your way through the hawser pipe! Well – isn't that a silly idea? He chuckles inwardly. Imagine anyone pinching a dip in the ocean from in between a lug of piping. That was no seaman's way.

No; he'll dive in, just ordinary, just as he was taught from the blonde wooden jetties of home. Just stand on the butts, then climb onto the bulwark. How many times had you done it as a boy and from a ship's side too if it must be known, a real back flipper into the harbor and off away down the road. Fuck their ships. Sure, of himself he shuffles eagerly towards the butts.

Yes, dive in; take a proper header!

To his ears comes the jumbled shouting of men. There is a commotion, the stamp of running feet, and a bellowing directed at him that is carried along on the wind.

'*What the blazes are you doing man? Get back on deck!*'

The startled officer makes a grab: '*Come back this minute,*' he orders. '*Come back!*'

'Think yourself smart do yeh, George Alexander smirks, coming to spoil me of a decent cooler. It's alright for him posted up on the bridge for his four hours and a drink of tea taken him every hour. You don't know what it's like to be roasted and soaked, on weevil biscuits and salted hog, on these your blasted Company ships.'

Then Mahoney is running at him; what the blazes is he doing here? The young seaman makes to grab him but with his smashed right hand and George Alexander has enough desperation in his sea legs to turn about and make him lunge and miss and hit his palm against the railings. He screams in pain.

'You are only going home he says to himself what is all the big fuss about? To be borne home on the soft waters of the Celtic Sea; is that being uncharitable?'

THE ROQUELLE

The Steam Schooner Roquelle built on the Clyde for Elder Dempster for the trade between Liverpool and the West African Coast. George Wailey jumped overboard into the Celtic Sea from this ship in July 1887 – his death was recorded as the result of 'severe malarial infection,' contracted after the vessel left Dakar.

He smiles. The useless devil of that black cat they all wonder at. Here is something real. You wave your hand at them and dive into the bosom of the ocean and wave again from the abyss of the waters. Fuck their ships.

On the bridge, all is bustle and excitement. The siren blazes out its raucous danger call. All hands dash on deck.

'Man overboard,' is the re-echoing cry. 'Man overboard! Stand By.'

George hears it all and laughs. You George Alexander Wailey hear it all. Do they think he's stupid, that he does not know about drowning or shipwreck after thirty-eight years at sea, Christ your life has been littered with the stuff?

He knows the story that after the lapse of a minute, or a minute and a half at the farthest, there supervenes a most peculiar kind of anguish. Nature then takes the management of your lungs into hers, and you breathe in spite of yourself, an action that has brought him clarity and peace in contrast to all the mad scramble for boats and siren blaring on the deck of that old lugger above him.

He takes a deep breath and finds himself adrift in the cool limitless water. This cold green light will carry him to Cork, standing at the bar, having a pint in the *Dragon* with his brother, another beautiful baby, like his own boys at home. Fuck that Conlan's brother Jerry.

The storm has blown away the clouds. You can see the lights, twinkling far over the Celtic Sea, the silver rays of the moon all around, the water shining in its black and silver glory.

He feels himself sinking; sinking deeper into the cool as a wave crests over him. He stops struggling for a moment to feel its healing balm and the great rim of the moon shines down as through a film of water as if sinking into the sea. It seems bigger and closer to the earth than you have ever witnessed from any ship; its energy would make any sinner look to heaven.

He can see Joe Conlan and the others, a smile not bitter but kind crosses his lips; God how you hope your own boys turn out as well, not a sneak thief like his brother, *Ah Well you can't help your family,* Bucko John and young George, William Patrick, Francis James and Henry the baby; Oh, and all your hopes that they would help us build an organization to assist all poor suckers cast adrift like their own poor Da.

He can no longer hear shouting from the lowered boat nor see the ship's lights bobbing on the water; could almost frame a smile from those lights, a smile as sweet as the sea itself and that of the cat, with its eyes like oil lamps that curse this old coffin box, even as it circles slowly around his slowly drowning body. Indeed !!! you say. His head sinks further from the stars. He is on his way home; home to embrace the ocean from where we all come and to where we all belong.

THE CREW OF THE PENTHSILEA

The Crew of the Penthsilea George sailed on in 1871, still working the American coast, seen here in the Puget Sound in 1905 after thirty eight years of trading and still carrying her Liverpool Registration even after having American owners for many years.

Ten

John Paul 1947 -
Going Away Again

They must have named you like this after your great uncle Johnny, but you didn't know that then. You didn't know anything. A family ruined by fire and water, and you have to go away; you John Paul who everyone calls Jackie has to get out of this, get off, that's how it starts when you set   sail on the *Barrister* fifteen years since birth and war in Liverpool. Then two months later, crates of lager later, buckets of slops later fed to the seagulls in Irish seas and Caribbean waters and lying drunk later, in sunsets, with mandrakes black as night diving into the purple twilight later: the ship turns and as slow as crickets whirr in the gathering dark, it brings you slowly home, the devil inside of all those who think they can escape by going away.

Drunken our Auntie who razes our house to the ground, fire, what the fuck do they know about fire; fire and water, the source of all our longings.

'God grant you some peace Jackie,' your ma says.

'We always seem to be fighting in this house.'

Home to Liverpool and the terrace up the coast, where at the bottom of the street, ships pass every day and with cups of tea and fags you'd sit dreaming Winter mornings, the old lady setting down a breakfast after the early shift delivering papers, moaning about the life drifting away from her and the old man out the front with his morning cough. Too much, too much of it tearing at you and instead turn the thoughts away, to brown Mexico and silver crucifixes and brass irons that stir the coals, that will solve all your problems, dance in the flames, a place of dreams.

'You'll travel the world Jackie, and you'll see what's there before you but never forget what you've left and how they all love you here.' That's his auntie talking.

Home to the Ocean city and just as soon away again; discharge book in pocket and imitated sailors clack of the paper rolled and beaten against the knee; you leave the train at Bank Hall and the stomach rises as the docks come in sight, and you remember the sweat and toil of that first lonely ship. Pathway to dreams broken on the back of second stewards and sneering shore-side cooks with their bets and big guts and later, secret calls in the night to women or boys; and 'Harry the Horse' who drives you through work in sinks and toilets within the desperate heat of the Caribbean. Drenched cotton vest as engineers leave their mark on shower walls, marks of a long apprenticeship and others not much older call you first tripper and ask where's your cherry and make passes at his balls.

What balls? Big and brave Jackie tells the cook he used to drink in the wine lodge down on Tarleton Street and hangs around Moorfields as if no one else knows and coughs dah-de-dah until he gets sick of Aussie Whites and knocks it on the head.

'Keep quiet you haven't done a trip yet.'

And put down, he can't speak where he's first learned to drink, down in the cellars with mates too young to go to the bar; so buy a few bottles then come back to Charley's and Fats Domino and Muddy Waters and Sleepy John Estes and all the old numbers of the Blues and arrive later to weave and stagger through golden summers and black winter Saturdays.

But they tell you keep quiet; keep quiet you fucken first tripper; first tripper, no tales to tell, no stories of crates of the stuff on birthdays and four of them, three bottles apiece, until they are crazy and swim out onto the fairground on the brickfield, lights in the sky beyond the dark river shot with purple across the rubble of the Wirral. Down to clubs that run without licenses 15 year old places full of drunks. Could not dance, could not dance, your legs tremble with the sober move but who gives a fuck when you're full of wine; whirling and spinning like a Catherine wheel and your head's like a rocket screaming out into the dark and girls, swaying like lanterns come wobbling out of the night.

None of that to tell, unbuttoning blouses and searching up skirts in entries and jiggers, the wet smothering mouth of kisses, skies still and soft and full of Autumn, rain and winds in Winter, little thoughts then of being away; only a girl from Waterloo letting him feel inside her knickers on separate Saturdays in the alley by the church; too cold to go to the beach, find a quiet corner. His mates telling stories of girls standing on bricks, then back to the club with the walls heaving and rumbling as they bulge and run with sweat. Fights break out in toilets and the group on stage asks for calm and then play on in a frenzy with their suits stuck to their skins and their arms up and stinking and their hair falling down while the dancers jump and blow and someone comes out with blood running onto his shirt and joins in with the music blaring and the whirling and twisting bodies throwing joints to the wind. The footballers gone wrong in such places, but none of that to tell, no notion of where he comes from, who his Dada is, why fire consumes him, no none of that, first tripper.

First tripper, the Friday you join the ship. Cabin decked out in wood, and winter sun over the docks splashes the cargo and filters through the porthole into the dark stain of the cabin, his new home, and it spills onto the table and the bunks stacked up in heavy plane and varnished brown. Thinking of that home as the ship comes through the lock gates of the half tide basin. A first introduction to the in between world of the sea and home: work in the Galleys and pantries and cabins; cards at night and maybe a drink, but all the time legends, nostalgia, reminiscences, stories of the future as flowing as the water in other times, other places, shifting as the tide that carries you downriver and water that is black as the difference between home and away until you realise that it's no distance at all.

Little of the now as they pass the Bar and make their way out to sea; Dirty George tells tales of the Orange lodge in the South end; old days, old families of grand masters and jobs on the southern docks, the southern mills or the Southern hospital for anyone who whistles the flute. The past always present for those with dynasties to protect and don't let anyone kid you that they only belong to the rich, the poor have their own way of decoding the message. Jimmy Whelan back where they live with a Rover outside the front door and a big television set in 1958 where Jackie and the old man sit watching the Manchester – Bolton final and eat thick ham sandwiches, and the old man and Jimmy drink bottles of Guinness and what a job Jimmy has with plenty of meat on the table and good cigarettes to smoke. And you ask the Da why doesn't he work on the docks and he just laughs and says some are always on the money and others come home week after week with fluff in their pockets. One of the first things you have to learn. You can't come in from the cold and dance the big time: not if nobody knows you; not in Liverpool.

THE BARRISTER

John Paul's first ship after sea training school in 1964; built in the 1950's for the Harrison Line she traded general cargo between Liverpool and the West Indies, the Gulf of Mexico and the Northern part of Latin America, Columbia, Guyana and Venezuela.

Harry the Horse doesn't like his pedigree; keeps you running all those months, running, cleaning, bringing up the stores. And the shouts, the curses and screams, his face an angry red flush; the woman he lives with how she never writes nor undresses in front of him when he's home. All these useless values, hopeless dreams, poor Harry suffering and drinking and nothing being what it is really about it all comes down on the first tripper. Harry, terrified of fire, locks himself away each night with his couple of cans , everything locked or knocked about with Harry and when you come home tired and pale and suffering, no-one knows if you have been near the sun and even fewer about that fire within you and what you don't even know you want..

Our Auntie the killer; the dockside dancer who runs the dance club and as the joints stiffen in the Liverpool air and the old, beautiful in her black clothes, Nana dies, takes easy to the drink, and is racked as much by the Pope as her arthritis and when the young lover starts to enter the back door of the old house, fights and shouts and the occasional scream when they come home after tiptoeing the boards and make their way through the kitchen where Uncle Billy waits with a knife . The old man coughing down the stairs to settle the uproar and remind them of the kids. Our auntie who sets the house ablaze in a whisky stupor one February night; a family on the street; the family split forever.

'The kid's communion suit ruined.' The old man looking up at the house as if at the pictures. The old lady crying, bitter futile tears.

'She's ruined everything, your auntie.'

Rooms in another, older, tiny place five minutes down towards the city. Roads full of holes and blocked entries and buildings with their roofs missing and the occasional woman stands on a corner by the pub; its own outhouse smashed since the war where she receives visitors; cold winter mornings, bright suns and skies and the frost still white on the brickfield; the old man in Walton Hospital with smoke in his lungs, like Uncle Billy, the start of their long careers. What does the Horse know about fire, locked up in his cabin every night, staring out at the darkness? What does he know about Dada's chest and blood in the cooper's sink every morning, ruined like the others in the smoke-filled workshops of the docks and Molly, the oldest auntie, only heard about from the Ma, dying from the red splinters shot from the raw glare of the metal box in 1931, fire and water, the ruin of Jackie's family.

Other pictures appear before him, visions of Mexico, cigarettes and tea and heavy eyelids and ripped wallpaper and feeling warm. Visions that make you sail under big red suns over mountains and muddy rivers and old brown quaysides. But first time ashore nobody asks if he wants to come with them ; fucken first tripper let him work it for himself. He has to carry his own proud standard; too make believe tough to ask for anyone's help. Fuck them fuck them all this miserable fucken crew; you'll go under your own steam and walk tall into the hot night.

Women sit on doorsteps and see a long wiry boy in tee shirt and jeans and call out laughing, all good humored as you walk, frightened but not wanting to show it up the alleys to bars and drink and company. Everywhere covered in hot dust and cloying heat as you pass the mission and the graveyard, the same stones where you come back later with a woman and think it safer for a knee-trembler under the stars; too scared to go to the brothel, full of smoke and black faces where they'll rob and kill you ; so come back here. She protests at sacred ground but pulls up her cotton skirt and you bend down, sweating and anxious and it's no good; too scared; your stage bravery won't pass muster here Jackie.

'Don't worry Honey.' She knows he's frightened and tries her best not to laugh.

No use, money in pocket she walks away humming a tune her teeth bright in the darkness; another fire behind him, far from the line of docks and wet cobblestone streets of the Liverpool waterfront where dust from the grain sheds turns to mud and spatters the green doors of warehouses in long muddy runnels and the gutters, the dock road that rings to second cooks singing *Strangers in the Night* in their mohair suits but it doesn't matter; it doesn't feel like failure and instead you're strangely proud, you stood up, you had a go ha ha, and fuck them all with their little clusters and cliques on board ship. You take a good drink that night out under the stars and within the folds of a bamboo bar.

Later, they carry you to your bunk after the watchman finds you collapsed in the alleyway besides the metal gangway, but you sing stronger now of yellow bars and purple nights full of rum. Banana boats and sugar boats and huddles of men, waiting to unload; older ones with white mufflers and grey faces. Liverpool air, the fire tears him away from Liverpool air into these nights full of stars and cicadas. Bragging next morning to others in the crew; bright yellow Caribbean morning, smells of molasses and coffee and Oh what a night!!!. Not wonderful, but you keep the story going and put a wild face on it and that evening you're out again walking the harbour streets of Barbados and with a spring in your step. This is great, you can do anything alone.

Clara Charles, never forget her. Sweetest woman of her house, quiet drink, a takeout half rum bottle wrapped in brown paper, smells from the gutter outside the window, baby in the back room sleeping. Tender woman shows you how while the sound of the street comes up on big saxophone notes and the baby lies there quiet in the cot. Women and sailors and the big world you come from breaking the little one's back, but there is none of that now, just a sweet lady and a Caribbean town and a purple sky and the lights on across the water and the drink making you feel warm inside and the fires that will take you to Mexico.

Hardly make the shore again. Too much work for everyone on this old hooker. When crew men pay off sick, someone has to pick up the slack and why not you first tripper; the Horse forever on your back and you watch the islands and quiet rivers of Venezuela only from the ship's rail as they constantly tie up and leave lonely wooden jetties with oil jibs that settle on the water.

Sundays with a quiet beer, and you sit on a tarpaulin hatch cover with old firemen, their prime gone and reflective enough to take in the young and one of them says, squinting through the sunlight at the shanty town of La Guardia sat on hilltops of corrugated iron and strewn with wood and white daub and down to the shimmering harbour where a speedboat cuts a swathe and slim brilliantined riders water-ski on sparkling water.

'That's the rich the world over; none of them give a fuck.'

He looks at his ingrained fingers as clean as he can make them for the Sabbath.

'How much do they see as they spin over other's lives?'

Liverpool the same; the old days and these firemen talk of tenement parties and meeting girls on landings and corners between floors where the sun hardly breaks and there's only one toilet apart from the jigger but always plenty of Guinness. Old streets pulled down not so long ago and Islington and Saint Anne's and Scotland Road is not the same as Huyton and Kirkby or Cantril Farm but it means more to them now, sat on the hatch looking over the Caribbean and the shanty town mountainside shimmering in the haze above, and down below on the water the eyes of the unseeing rich; blind the world over. The Horse calls out again and starts his shouting, his face flushed red with every frustrated sinew. What does he know?

And the fireman and the donkey man drink and sit back on the deck in the sunlight; too old now to be ashore and thinking already of home when the city means more to them than it did years before. Quiet days for reflections not even the rich can disturb. The easy sun of late Sunday afternoon. Clean white vests protecting the shoulders and paunches held in by the faded overalls and calm with the drink they can even talk to the young.

The houses come on down and the people move away, but they keep on talking and remembering and sometimes even hoping; and the dullest of days and the weather changing from sun to cloud only finds them with a wry smile and the increasing sureness of another trip completed as the sea turns from the colour of green to black glass and the lights wink out from Cabo Vincente and Finisterre and the radio comes clear out of the Celtic Sea and sometimes you think they don't know where they are or even if they care.

You with hair plastered down and fragrant drops from a bottle of aftershave smarting on the chin as they come up river in the rain; you're full of life, polishing the last of the wood and the brass burnished and gleaming under the dull sky for the gaze of company superintendents: everything for the Captain when you're away; everything for the owners when you're at home; and everyone dances to the tune. Captains turn to jelly and superintendent's tremble when some doddery old remnant of the owner's family hobbles aboard.

The crowd down below only litter this horizon and radios are turned up and new tunes welcome them home, and no one thinks of going back again amongst the ruins of the city; the same old smells and the falling rain and you think it would all be here forever until someone tells you different. And with every day passing, you say only one more to go until two months have gone by, and you welcome the shadows of the dock road and long at the same time to be away. What does it matter if you're dancing the same tune as everyone around here?

But the ease, the ferocious ease of those few minutes when the last jobs are finished, down in the wooden cabin, books jammed between mattress and bunk, tea and tobacco tin on the table, strains from the radio in the unholy quiet, slow turning engines waiting to be stilled. Waiting quietly as the ship draws alongside and you make a cigarette. Then the calm shatters as ropes are thrown ashore and gangway lowered, and heavy boots come clambering over the steel. Nothing like a ship docking in her hometown, trip completed; the bang and clatter of customs' men, dockers, watchmen all coming up the gangway searching for food and drink; it all feels like you have been here before but with something gone missing.

Dirty boots everywhere; customs in boiler suits prising behind cupboards and glass backs heaving trays of sandwiches to put them off the scent. And surprise, surprise, don't find anything, the boss has already been paid off; the pay-off replacements. Everyone wanting the 'dropsy' when the ship comes home, officials, superintendents, the union, tailors and chandlers, runners with bundles of cloth; fuming store managers for whom every ship is late, all making anywhere for where they can get a drink and down below it flows like water; the night watchmen are smiling; all of them in those first few hours, stewards and cooks, deck-hands and greasers, engineers and dockers tilting the throat, singing the tunes, a home ship in her home port.

To clean and scrape and wash like that and have it all ruined; boots thud down alleyways and dockers crash against gleaming bulkheads; this old coffin box stripped and polished and chipped in long hours of sunshine and sweat is now filthy within a moment and only clean again when she's back at sea. It's just another wheeze, just another run, part of the crack to have no-one see the blood or scrubbed alleyways or coughed up dust from the engine room and boilers except to know it's your turn next, like any first voyage, never the same again, like the burn in your Dada's throat, the lump in Uncle Billy's lungs, your aunties hot hands and dancing feet.

'Done a trip have you la'?'

And Liverpool now a rainbow of cranes and concrete; Jackie coming home with a mist on the river that hovers over the line of docks that pass on the electric train. The old terraces are dying, idle with the slates missing and the slats showing through; rotten wood, but where people have made their homes, slumped in the seat gazing through the beads of mist at berths and ships and wondering if he has what it takes to do the same again. Looking around, where bulldozers throw up black bricks into the air and the smoke and dust rise in little clouds from the ruined, beautiful city.

He's not so sure.

Put it out of mind; can think too much so sit in the all-night club's wine and beer inside you; hush puppies and red socks fired up and gangling on uppers. 'Rattling' they call it, and the music playing low at four in the morning and the dreams coming up that end with the dawn, the life of Liverpool as it looks ever West. Yankee bars and wine lodges and ferries across the river to the 'One-eyed city' and further to North Wales where on early holidays you sit amidst the crowds and watch the ships coming upriver with gold on their rusted decks.

The sun on brown oily water peered at through windows of the old Overhead; rotunda boxing clubs and tales of Marciano and La Motta recounted by your Da, always larger always bigger somehow in this city; a place always on the lookout, on the move, always going somewhere; a sharpness that belongs to generations of casual workers, closed parishes and far horizons and very different from the stolid Lancashire hinterland. A place all its own, full of comers and goers; a city of the water near and far that knows more of Brooklyn and Baltimore and Boston than it does of Bury or Blackburn or Burnley.

Years back, riding the brown boxcars of the Overhead with the old man, yellow and black shadows moving between the iron stanchions, the old man marvels at the raging sunset across Seaforth and the ships coming off the Bar and beyond that the Irish Sea.

'Night watchmen are the city's soul son. They have seen the wind and want nothing more than to sip tea and take the occasional big drink. Always give them a few coppers when you have it son, it fuels their visions.'

Discharge book in pocket and nervous now as docks come in sight; passing streets and remembered Christmases long past with the Nana and the great aunties and scattered distant cousins always on your mother's side and Uncle Con Rogan singing *Kevin Barry* and the old man murdering *Danny Boy*, and sixteen rums for his cold that late December night, full of shandy and sips of brown beer, and hearing quarrels of how many Irish died in the making of the docks and shipyards and tunnels; a city built on slaves and immigrants; then sleep and wake wrapped up in blankets in the back of a taxi held by the old man through the yellow dark of a coming year.

Where are you now, on this busy dockside with a Spring wind cracking a dull day and office girls with

flowers on their dresses and a few old-timers at Bank
Hall with blackened teeth and hands that shake as
they puff on stubs, nervous as sleep-walkers blind men
selling matches; more, always more as you come near
the river and hear the roar of the in between streets
full of workshops and hope and broken lives that lead
down to the ships.

Over there, you can see the Blue Star boats that stand
out amongst the tangle of derricks, their funnels
between steel and wood and the Pacific Steam that
go to Valparaiso and up the coast to Antofagasta then
back down to Montevideo and Buenos Aires. Further along the blackened escarpments, Cunard boats
tower over the whorls and turrets of nineteenth century gateposts; pale stone sculptures thrown in relief
that mirror the rusted slings on warehouses and high
haylofts with jutting prongs for mailbags that used to
be discharged on hooks. Ships, all waiting for crews
to join, to sign up, to leave, to be away, Cunard Yanks,
Hungry Harrisons, Blue Funnell, and the ever-present
Welsh Marine where a century before on another stage
George Edwards, spat his denouncements to a booing
jeering crowd when he appeared drunk on the boards
of the theatre.

'I'll play no more to this wretched town and its cargoes enslaved when born. Where every brick of its buildings is stained in the blood of the poor.'

And you, nervous now as the berth comes in sight and you see gangs of young dockers, warehousemen, ships stores and apprentice mechanics playing football in the cobblestone alleys in the shadows of the blackened warehouses. The train shudders and stops and you wonder what another trip will bring; if the old hooker will she have you back again, the barnacled sweatshop on her way down to Mexico in the coming weeks, will she take you to the bright blue washed mornings of Vera Cruz ; the fear within as you walk aboard and into the dull orange light of the galley but instead of sneering the crowd greet you as though you're one of them; they drink their coffee, light up cigarettes, even joke with you all the way out to the deck as if the last trip has never been.

The fear off you now; you've already *done one in her* and can laugh at the old sentiments from last trip but instead of Mexico and dreams of silver coastlines and dancing women you're assailed by a servant from the superintendent's Office who tells you you're wanted there and to make for the Harrisons building on the main Canada Dock.

'Go and pack your bag Jackie,' says one of the bosses. 'You'll be off on the morning tide; sailing on the pride of the fleet for the Republic of South Africa.'

Little time to swallow, to cough or protest, the greatest rebel runs messages sometimes. You do what you're told, crestfallen and strangely ashamed that you've betrayed the dream and hopes of the muddy brown of Mexico, but a small consolation is you've escaped the Horse; the hooker was his ship and he was going nowhere.

Sunday evening away to the Cape, the cook is on deck and you, the sailor's Peggy, hang around the galley waiting for the pans and dixies to take below for the able bodied seamen. The sun's out and lowering and the sea is as green as peppers with slow white-caps gently turning in scrolls and the evening comes down all lilac and purple like the ancient maps in the captain's cabin. The dusk replaces the sunny wooden stateroom with the swish of the water beyond the glass with a light that crosses the ocean and is the colour of golden dust and the cook turns around and says.

'You're fucked in this game sonny. When you look out like this you think of home, and when you sit in the armchair with the television on and a big tea inside you.' He waves his dumpy little arm 'all you can think of is this.'

Not too soft though' he lights a cigarette and coughs and gobs over the side and shouts to the Galley boy to get on with it as the shadows lengthen along the deck.

Then with the sun gone and the breeze turning chill, one shadow stays longer and wants to chat as they enter the steaming showers and you have to look sharp to see the old glitter of lust come up in the eyes. Wine Lodge romance they call it. You dry yourself and cut out quick and tell the galley-boy to do the same, but he's slower and wants to stay to make his own peace.

Later, changed and brushed, you go down to the pantry and pass his cabin but no-one's there. You can still hear the shower and press an ear to the locked door. You hear the bump and groan from behind the sharp hiss of water and see the boy later and his face has got that vacant expression the newly deaf carry and he starts crying within the embarrassed silence, and you can't do much more except bring him tea and give him a smoke and add more thought to the stories of the in-between world, the curious flow, the keepers of such dreams.

A change of atmosphere like a change of address or an uprooted home and seamen the archetypes of this limbo world bring other mish-mash of stops and starts that haunt anyone who has been away; illuminate them as are only the lightning struck in their own static dance and you hear The Auntie whisper to herself amidst all the fears that would consume her.

'Another Catholic soul gone to the wind.'

Eleven

Going ashore, pea coat buttoned down in the Cape Winter and dancing in the Bar Delmonico full of brandy sours, the girls on the floor throw their arms out and call for the shout. Seamen watching silently over their drinks, when to make a move, when to stay, who to watch and as the night goes on, one gets up weaves his way across the floor to ask a favour; perhaps a fine waltz of hope, silently, others join him.

'Everyone has their time sonny. Everyone.' someone says in a quiet whisper.

But all around the Cape there is a strange emptiness and harshness. The overseers on the ships in their khaki shorts and Sam Browne belts buckled near the gun. And on late Saturday where a wind is blowing down the road passed the Mission and the white men are drinking in the Orangeboom bar and talking sport, and down the road across from the pickup trucks and gleaming motor bikes, you see a black man with no shoes, and the wind is kicking up the dust and blowing it down to the bay, and he's sat there on the curbside, drunk with his head in his hands and his piss running away into the gutter, through the orange peel and peanut shells and cars passing by that holler out their scorn.

Forget that as the ship moves her way around the coast, through Port Elizabeth and Durban, where the white buildings come down to the ocean and the clubs are classier than Cape Town but you don't like it, you want to be back in the Caribbean or on the way to Vera Cruz; not this industrial republic built on slaves. And the Yarpies, the Afrikaners, a miserable, hard fucking lot who'd eat you or shoot you if they got the chance. And hate the liberal Europeans, hate everyone if the girls pause or ignore them, or do them no favours while they give everything to these fucking dancing seamen.

Glad to leave the constant fighting and miserable drinking of two months on that coast. Casting off from Cape Town on a cold Saturday afternoon, the harbour quiet and a heavy blue-sky overhead; water slapping against the side of the quay and the flat sandy hinterland stretches away beyond the harbour. Glad that the ship is leaving this coast. Glad that you are leaving these ports, a no-man's land of scrub and desert where white men wear pressed Terylene trousers and their women blue dresses and parade with perfume along the sole strip of the shopping street carved out of the bush.

All around looming grey clouds are obscuring the sky across huge flat stretches of water and quietness and the Blacks melt away into thin air; away to their townships on the outskirts, away to homes where they have no home. And ropes fall away from the ship's side and bobble on the water and the pilot calls out and you edge away leaving behind the light of the Republic and the empty streets and the scraps of paper caught and flung by the wind, 'the land of good hope,' says one, as they bucket the rollers around the Cape, the land of no fucking hope.

How can you just leave this as the ship's after-end swings around and the Bow points towards the outer harbour; your last stop before the Irish Sea and nothing but Ocean for four lonely weeks, and at the last moment someone has caught your gaze on the starboard side and points to his head and says simply.

'Don't forget us man.'

It hangs on you amidst the cleaning and the cooking day after day and it's snowing and it's cold off the anchor outside Belfast after twenty-six lonely watches at sea and everywhere is shining again after weeks of good sleeping weather, eating, washing and scrubbing and passageways gleam for the home ports. You turn again that night on the anchor and the radio is playing the Beatles on a set the second cook has brought to the empty scrubbed down galley and the wind bangs through the sea door from the open deck and the notes of *Michelle* carry on the air while it rages across the Irish Sea and the cook says, 'What the fuck are we doing here.' Forget, how can you forget?

Back in Liverpool, the new rating in hand, you buy a few pints and share jokes in the Irish club in the late afternoon, where dockers vie with seamen as to who could drink the most before going back to ships or quayside . Others look on in their suede, black vestments and dog collars, to whom such consider-ations bore little importance, blessed as they are in the provinces of the soul. And the drink slides down and the talk becomes louder and smoke thicker and you drift away inside , a wry smile crossing the lips, and think how smart you've been. You have the tag now, they'd taken your promised voyage to Mexico away; but it was worth the swap even a couple of trips to that fucking republic. Drink does that but now you have the number and can travel from ship to ship as a journeyman with wages more than double than that of the galley boy or a kid delivering dixies to the seamen; a Peggy. You're on your own now and have to make your own way and the crew are less forgiving and you soon find that out in Glasgow. The sea a circle for all his days.

Glasgow in the winter, with the tenements coming down to the dock and tired clusters of women with faces slashed by razors and jagged lipstick sit in Betty's Bar or by Jeannie's on Plantation Quay and the Gorbals screams the Irish question but provides no answers, only a way of life with The Celtic scrawled on the sides of newly painted ships and 'Fuck the Pope' on the yard walls hammering and roaring down the Clyde.

Another second steward, another Horse tries to screw you like in those first stormy days and nights at sea but you're older now and have done a trip but that other part of you is still exposed, turned outward and shown, cruel in the winter light. Nothing like going away to do that to you: and when you're asked for drink after the pubs have closed ,you'll give none away on a sad, cold and closed down Sunday afternoon. Only a can or two for himself that a sweet girl from Drumchapel has left except she hasn't shown up again. You sit alone in the lonely cabin gazing out into the grey afternoon light; a quiet lager and a smoke on the empty ship, a hulk without a soul, engines stilled and footsteps like stones echoing in the alleyways.

'We always thought your sermons were great Father Jim, didn't we Jackie?'

The Auntie's hand tugs the bottom of the young priest's jacket. She turns and grins at you.

'Never be afraid love, there's nothing here to scare us.'

'You don't want to be telling him that,' the priest grins.

The second steward hammers on the door for drink as you sit miserable in this quiet, cold City with no woman nor workers to liven the quays. Pull the cabin port light down to ignore him and shame upon shame, turn the key quietly in the lock. You're miserable enough without giving away any last drops to an angry juicer.

The steward catches you, his eye bulging as you close the port and you sit alone, sad-faced and drinking the last drops. Swears he will have you. Swears he'll bust your balls on this and every ship and stamps his boots down on the iron deck and cracks at the iron panel with the palm of his hand.

'You've fucken had it la !!!'

And all that week as they steam out of port and down the West coast , he is at his elbow with shit that he would not bother another soul with; showing him up in front of the other seamen and making him look bad with his new rating as if he got that by thieving too. The name of tight arse on all the lips of his drinking buddies; a locker of doors, a scrivener, the worst label you could bear aboard a ship.

And you try to ride it out, a lousy drop of lager and you have to face this shit; stoic and stupid and woman-less, sad to be acting brave, sitting it out in the falling light whiles the curses and threats and epithets roll down the deck and empty alleys ring with it.

'Am going to fucken burst you.'

An abuse that continues at sea and on rivers all around the West and you have to stay numb, thinking on the new ticket and bad blood in the ship and what any new trip this is going to be like with the first shrouds of responsibility thrust upon you. And worse, the ship is going to that beloved Mexico, where the only brown visions will hang out his shame and sorrow surround him like a crown of thorns.

A Friday afternoon Liverpool and the bosses are away to their pubs and clubs. A docker appears in a shaft of light from the forward hatch and offers Jackie and the Galley Boy a bottle of fine Oban whisky going cheap. Too late for the pub, they've been left to load stores that the Second should have attended to but that's all part of his stunts. They sit in the cabin and swill down the pale-yellow spirits in white tooth mugs, light up constant cigarettes and tell themselves this is great.

By the time of the turn-to, the bottle is empty, and their faces red as traffic lights against a grey wooden afternoon and there's nothing much to do except hang around the pantry and wait the dreaded moment when the man and his mates come back from the pub. The steward bursts in. He's worse than the Horse with his temper, his lost keys, his fears, and vindictiveness. He asks the boy studiously polite. Others have seen no keys. He has a bad look on him and turns to Jackie, eyes full of fury; venom spitting off his tongue.

'And you, you tight cunt where are the fucking things?' He explodes.

His face is livid and up close to your face. The smell of the pints and tobacco enclose him. You have had enough. Bad blood in the ship be arsed, whisky brave you stick one on him.

Now this feller says he is a hard man from a hard family in the North end and Jackie has no pedigree, no brothers away at sea, no dockers living, no history so the Horse has told you, but the Horse is scared of fire and Jackie knows more about that than anyone. And once you're exposed, you're exposed for good, and hard men always carry that risk.

Bad spirits have surrounded the deck all week, raised and heightened in you by the whisky. After that first maddened blow you are soothed by a raw calm. You land another good shot on his nose and he goes down and makes a great clatter with the falling pans by the shining server press. The sound of running is heard down the alleyways and visions of murder and laughter echo on the air; then the steward's body seems to roll under the press with only his head with its crinkled hair and bald patches pointing out from under the steel and Jackie lets him have it again, this time with the hooves.

The week has taken its toll, all thoughts of restraint gone now, you stick him in hurried, shuffled stabs before heavy boots pour into the pantry and arms pull you away. He reckons he is a hard man and he comes alive after that initial surprise has laid him low. The third mate is holding his precious keys to the storeroom, the magic keys that has brought them to all this... The Steward tears them from him.

'Get down to the there and we'll sort this fucking thing out.'

There is murder in his voice. Engineers and fitters are all over the pantry deck by now. AB's stand around smiling; dockers and greasers have been brought to the spot. The captain is away; The Chief is entertaining in his quarters. One lowly Mate, hardly out of his time as midshipman tries to assert authority and is ignored. This is a ship in her home port.

'Get down to that fucking store-room,' the second steward screams again; the arena of close quarter fighting.

His face is bleeding but it's the shame more than anything that ignites him.; this tight cunt has stuck one on him and he's going to pay. Someone passes him a handkerchief. He tosses it aside and it flutters to the deck. Bad blood in the ship or not, the question has to be settled. Someone tries to issue a command.

'This is mutiny,' wails a young engineer, wallowing back from the pub.

'Refusing orders,' a docker breaks in with a smile.

'Fuck your orders,' his mate answers him, 'this is better than the Stadium.'

Friday afternoon in the Liverpool docks, rain, mud, the smell of grain, anyone with any sense away home to their families, only workers filling in their time. The second steward who is called Rinty by his mates grabs Jackie and the dance starts again.

'Rebellion,' someone shouts. A greaser boils up the kettle. Everyone is a corner man now.

You watch your step all the way far down below where the stores are kept in a cool red painted cellar and when he swings in front of you to make the last flight his own, you think about kicking him down the rest of the way but the thought of never sleeping easy passes through your mind.

Tales of others flood through you who have held the initial surprise but have lived to regret it when black revenge is visited upon them months later while they lay sleeping. You don't need that; you want Mexico and silver crosses and easy visions. The storeroom door creaks open, and crashes closed, and you know you're in a scrap.

All surprise gone you feel yourself trembling in the time it has taken for the first furious burst to cool, and the fury has to be fanned alight again. Rinty comes on fast and catches you with a hard right and another couple and tries to take you down. Now was his time. Inch by inch he tries to turn you and pull you under, a death roll, but you hold on. A wriggle of the neck and a shuffle like you'd been taught after football, and you suddenly feel one arm free; the other still locked around the neck of the second steward. Liberty. You smash that white orb of a face; pound at it and it does not last much longer; Rinty's eyes tell you that.

'Enough,' he croaks.

He puts his arm around you to make himself look good as you come back up the ladder. The greaser gives them a cup of tea. Rinty's face is lumpy and red, bruises everywhere around the eyes. His smile gives the game away. You don't give a fuck; the bastard would be off his back now. A docker gives you a roll-up and you smoke and drink the hot, sweet tea. A young seaman looks happy; not so much at the outcome but the way officers have been shouted down.

'See the way we fucked them off,' he says to the old greaser who hands out mugs as if they were at the Rotunda.

'Don't be at it,' the old man nods in the direction of the departing officers.

'They always clear out of the way when you want to knock one of your own around.'

You tell them that the bastard has been on your back for weeks.

'Same difference, they can tolerate that, keeping it all between youse; that's how they run this game, how they run the Army. That's how the owners run them. Down there for dancing son,' and he gives a little shuffle.

You listen, keep it all in mind when they shake hands and agree to sail. No bad blood in the ship. The Caribbean suns and the brown soil of Mexico greet them after ten days away from the Mersey and you laugh and dance and drink and think you've made it and sleep with black women and brown women and don't care much for anything as time goes by on the fastest of trips, with chickens scratching in the dusty streets and wooden fires made on the quayside and sojourns down long blue and white avenues with music playing everywhere and taxi drivers blaring their horns and kissing their wooden crucifixes that dangle and bounce above the steering wheels in all the great strength and hopelessness of the Mexican ports that mix everything together with laughter or hopeless disdain.

Far from the soulless Cape there is something different here that you always knew existed, a journey of waiting on time and time standing still and people living within its clear light; nights strung with lanterns, sawdust and drink and people dancing out their lives in one great howl.

On the return from Vera Cruz and Matamoros they stop at the Cayman Islands to load Bacardi rum on one quiet sunlit evening off Nassau. They ride at anchor under a golden sky waiting for the barges to come. Seven hundred cases of the stuff bound for Liverpool and a whole crew is watching with a wary eye, an easy drink, a scouse party.

'You have to seize your time son,' his auntie says at the hospital. Uncle Billy with the tubes all down him and not able to speak and her waltzing around, giving off her perfume and her shiny dancing dress billowing out all ready for the Grafton.

'Seize your moments, Jackie. They'll call you to hell but seize them just the same.'

Uncle Billy's eyes look longingly at her, like two black stones above the sheets.

Eddy signals the move when the officers have broken for their tea. You throw down two shirts to a docker in the hold and he looks around, rubs his yellow vest and passes up two bottles. Other faces appear above the rim of the hatch and do the same and soon money and cheap watches, rings and clothes flood down on the gang and one yellow case with that distinctive red and black stamp makes its way slowly up the hold, followed by another and another as the money keeps raining down; the embossed stamp on the boxes a lux-urious sealed emblem of the old Cubano days are now shining for this Liverpool crew who always know how to dance, and all the way home cabin parties replace the quietness of sea sleeps and the relentless pistons.

Consumption of lime juice soars, but the chief steward does not worry, he has his share; When the Captain enquires about the rate of consumption, he answers.

'The men are worried about a bout of scurvy sir .'

The crew are the only ones who must steal but that is Eddy talking and everyone knows his number. You sit around and listen to him recount the seaman's history and the things you must do outside of yourself. Eddy has been away since the middle fifties and has taken his part in that turn of the decade year when democracy becomes the order of the day and a union now existing as a company shop since its own revolutionary beginnings starts to feel the pressure from below.

'It was great,' he says 'the ships all idle in the dock in that June and September of 1960. We came out twice that summer and that took some doing but we showed them and even if the settlement was no good, we made some changes, and more are on the way.'

Spud Magee goes below to search for a case of Heinz beans amidst the night-time talking and the wind, gentle off Ireland, and brings back to the deck his newspaper cuttings as well as a few cans. The shadows of that year peer out crumpled in black and white lines and even the 'quality papers' talk about unofficial movements in the union 'that for too long has been resting on its oars.'

'The papers said that?'

'Damn right,' says Spud, 'and they'll say a whole lot more if they think they're on the hook, same as the one's that run this game now.'

Eddy laughs and tucks into his beans. He says,

'Why didn't you take up with the union Spud?' And Spud says, 'they didn't want to know me, too much of an old arse; too long a casual, a bum, a sea lawyer who'd sign none of their contracts after the war.'

He smiles again, solid. Solid as a thousand others who have passed through and moved on; and says he's too old now and tired but that doesn't mean he still hasn't got the anger.

'But everyone has their time sonny,' he says. 'Everyone. I've had mine and you'll have yours.'

Twelve

Now you've come to stand on the stones in the quiet light of Summer. Stand there now on the dock road, the warehouses, shimmering black in the sunlight and throwing shadows across the water where the rubble of the Wirral rises out beyond the locks and you hold up the placard that says *40 hours* and an odd lorry goes by and kicks up the dust and the driver sometimes waves.

Young unsure, you look over at the ships all laid up in their berths and thinks of how dead they look no more than rusting iron hulks without the men. And the coppers look out from their hut as they stroll up and down and you try to remember how it all starts, and it is funny how he can't; can't remember anything except walking up and down on the picket line each Friday as if he had been doing it all his life and forgets the time he didn't bother.

You cast your mind back to the song, the only song that Eddy knew and you picture him there that night with his hair blowing and his fists up and the sound of *The Saints* going rolling around the deck, and his voice saying 'Don't let them fool you,' his voice rising and falling and then becoming lost in the wind. And now it's a quiet afternoon in late May and no one goes up the gangway anymore and still the song dances in your head.

Months passed. Eddy would sit in his cabin and stare at the radio that gleamed back at him from the small alcove. The set with its little buttons and dials and rich leather casing meant more than anything to him when he was away. Bought in New York, polished every day, stations that make him happy.

'It's the connection,' he says.

With his watch finished he'd sit and tune in, listening to the different bursts of music and voices that somehow kept him in touch. Connects him to the American Services, Blues, Jazz, Tamla-Motown when you hit the Caribbean; Eddy has a girl in Grenada who dances to the same tunes. She used to call for him on Sundays down at the quay and off he'd go, showered and shoes shining, running down the plank and waving to those bastards spending their lives stooped and working overtime: mortgaged lives out on the deck but all that has stopped since the deal and now you have to work seven days a week.

'Is that your stomach rumbling Jackie? Are you taking communion love?'

At mass, the seven o'clock morning shift; her eyes are as laden as an overloaded barge with lack of sleep and Saturday night's cargo.

'I've always found a dab of scent makes all the difference to settle you.'

And she shakes a drop from a little square bottle right there at his shoulder right in front of the old biddies.

'Look after your soul Jackie, no matter what.'

The radio plays slow, Eddy wonders why his girl doesn't come down anymore. Another man; another dear John; he has to work Sundays? His only freedoms are the few hours at night. He jiggles with the dials and the music comes roaring out. It isn't enough for them to have you on their bastard ships all your life; they want your days to boot. He sits down, suddenly still and thinks of all the moments they chisel out of him as if he's made of stone.

And the days turn from blue to grey and they come back to the wide Atlantic. You sit in Eddy's cabin and talk about different things and the people they'd sailed with and listen to the radio and the wind blow fierce to Starboard. One time he's tuned to the World Service, and they hear that the union are not too happy with the way they have to work the extra hours without overtime or any choice after the last deal and Billy Conlan shrugs and says if they feel like that why did the bastards agree to it in the first place. Eddy shakes his head and gets out the last of the bottle.

Back home you get the drift of the way things are moving down at the union. Most of the Liverpool branch want to get back to the idea of the forty-hour week and Conlan, ever the sceptic, raises his whiskers from out of his glass and says they've been talking about that since he's first come away. And Jackie keeps quiet, what with everything that has happened in the last year since his rating and bears it all in mind without knowing really what way to think, except that the notion of tight arse is behind him.

Then they are sailing high on the Caribbean again. The great island harbours wash away those lonely days on the African coast, and within him now as the days pass in song and the nights a blur of music in the sheer ferocious ease. The skipper hasn't turned out bad and Saint Lucia and Saint Kitts and Antigua and

Barbados roll pass like a dream and then down to the blue waters of The Grenadines and Eddy's girlfriend, returns in full flood, comes down in her car one night and takes a crowd of you way up on the high road. Beyond the trees and scrub, the water glistens below like a blue jewel. Parched lips turned to tilt to the necks of dancers whirling in the midst of the island clubs and someone gives you a weed to smoke and makes your head go light and by Christ, he doesn't want to know about anything except the music and dancers jumping and twisting and twirling.

You get up and sing and do a little piece and people are laughing and clapping , their eyes rolling like dice and you see Eddy and his girl with their faces closed in the dark and dancing slow while everywhere else is turning and bobbing and banging and the drink keeps flowing, and Jackie doesn't know what he's taking any more; and next morning, with his head like a cathedral bell and a stomach on his knees, the cook calls down the alleyway for breakfast and shouts to everyone the union have called a strike. Homeward bound, they hear that the Prime Minister is going to speak to all seamen on the radio, and down you go to the mess deck and sit next to Jimmy Cavanagh and Barney Hayes who have come from the galley and tell him the officers' mess is full and every bastard there that a strike won't affect anyway.

And next they know, the room goes quiet and the seamen pull up their chairs and Premier Wilson's slow Yorkshire accent comes filtering out over the room in such a tone they think the green rollers of the sea are going to turn back; it's so solemn. And it halters on and on, saying what good fellows they all are and how the nation owes them a great debt, but is heavily in debt herself and at this time of crisis, how seamen are more than valuable.

Some of the crew are nodding and others are just sitting there quiet as the voice grows more firm and decisive and warns of what harm a strike will do and the margin of the balance of payments and that seamen do not want to be responsible for holding the nation to ransom; the voice trails on and on, laying down point after point, until it lacquers the very stools and chairs they sit on and covers every inch of the wooden bulkheads and has everyone rooted until its presence slowly fades and there is silence in the mess.

No one says a word and blokes if they look at you simply raise their eyes or give little embarrassed smiles and it's hard to know what anyone is really thinking. Some scrape their chairs against the deck as they lean back, hands behind their heads; others roll smokes and light them before they start to drift away and if you haven't the feeling before, you have it then, that the message has sunk home and no-one really knows what to do so they smile or smoke to hide their silence.

Then a funny thing happens, Eddy sings his song. A party some days later and everyone has brought their cans until they spill over and fill the deck of the Customs' room. People are perched on the double bunks and others bring in stools to balance on and one, searching for an opener, pulls a wedged locker open and there stands in proud isolation three bottles of Bacardi some bastard has filched and forgotten the previous trip. You sit there and chase the spirits with lager, the smoke becomes thicker and the songs louder, the Bosun comes knocking, he cannot sleep. Out of the steaming cabin someone has got hold of a tea chest and fixes a brush pole up with cord to bung, bung, bung on the base, and another brings out the spoons and everyone breaks into the sash, and you all go trooping down the alleyways limping and laughing and blowing on imaginary flutes the way they do for the *Glorious Twelfth*.

'*That'll do him, the moanin' fucker.*'

And out on the after-end, with the wind blowing and clouds riding like mountains across the moon, you continue with the music and the watchmen just finished come to join and cabins are ransacked for any last drop. Then when the heads are rolling and the base has gone quiet and the only sound is the ocean roaring down the runnels, Eddy weaves himself up onto the hatch; his hair blowing wild and hands dangling by his sides like you see in the movies. He's mumbling something about all us poor bastards throwing our lives away and then starts singing the only rebel song he knows and his head is shaking and then the *Saints* goes billowing around the deck. You're all up on your feet giving it the last turn when he crumples his hands into fists above him and as the strains go gliding off into the night as he waves them about and shouts above the wind and sound of the ocean.

'Don't let them fool you,' and louder 'Don't let the bastards fool you.'

The song keeps dancing in your head all the way home, and you can tell even in those early days there's something going on by the way ships are being laid up in the berths. And after they come through the blackened locks and wait for their pay Jackie goes up through the gates, passed the lines of warehouses and trucks and coiled ropes and slogans of the lonely pickets and the thought of standing there, murdering his time makes him want to run; but he's down in the union some days later and they say they need someone for the Sandon gates, and before he knows it he's standing there with his board by the quiet dock; the coppers watching them from their hut and the odd lorry passing and the driver sometimes waving his arms or tooting and the wheels in the sunlight kicking up the dust.

The days go by slowly, broken only by returning ships, and you would meander along to see if you knew anyone and maybe have a drink and a few smokes. And the union is organised alright, every day they have a crowd up at Canning Place, register them and dispatch the pickets and those with a few bob would hang around and if you knew them buy you an entrance. Other times you'd have one in the Animal House that Jimmy Cavanagh's auntie used to run, and when the money ran short, she would always let you have a few and pay her when you could, strike or no strike.

Days drags by into weeks and Jackie keeps on doing his turn; hanging around by the gates, talking to the old ships' watchmen who can remember that the strikes were never legal and always broken back in their own time, watching the ships strung side by side across the water with their flags and colours bursting the docks and wondering how many blokes were just like him, the sun pouring down and the glare and dust of the pavements turning the throat sour in the unreal silences that stretch the length of the dock road.

And he meets Ronnie Ferguson one day and the two little kids he has with him are screaming the place down. He looks like he's going to go mad until Jackie buys ice-cream and everything returns to quiet. Pay and the pain goes away, that's what The Auntie used to say. And seeing it's the North end they keep watch outside the Gladstone dock and Jackie goes back with him for a cup of tea and walks through streets he's lived on ten years before and sees little difference in the brickfields and holes in the road left by the war or any other traces of where The Auntie has burned their house.

You sense his place is worse as soon as you cross the door, the curtains drawn even as the sun belts down. Three little children are sitting in the gloom, another bundle on the wife's knee. Jackie looks at the woman's red hands and furrowed features as she brushes the lank hair away from her face and turns her eyes as Ferguson goes out to make tea and she calls after him there is none, and no child supplement until the morning. He looks as if he's going to shout as colour floods his face and the kids look at him and start crying but the wife comforts and strokes them and shoos the eldest back to the streets and into the sunlight and looks back at her husband with an angry glare.

You catch one of them to go and buy some tea and other pieces and the wife takes a smoke, and it rises around the room while the sun cracks the flags outside and she asks how long will it last and you say you don't know and take a disguised breath and wonders why he doesn't seem to know anything. You look from the linseed cloth on the table to the torn linoleum floor and smell the fuggy smell of bedroom clothes the kids are wearing and imagines the nights in this heat with them all whimpering and moving and scratching on the mattresses and Ronnie next to his worn out woman, her worried face with what to feed them and the lousy few bob from the supplement and the even fewer shillings from the union.

'Tell him to take his kids away with him down there.' She nods to the river.

Anything to get them from under her feet for a few hours; bad enough when he's away, but at least she has a bit of time to herself, the allotment note is regular, and she can make ends meet.

'Him,' she laughs her scorn, 'coming home with his brothers, drunk, a few groceries or a fish wrapped up in paper, what does that do?'

Jackie shakes his head and can't answer and meets Ferguson's half smile and leaves his cigarettes and takes big breaths in the street outside and calls out goodbye as the kids range loose on the brickfield amidst the twinkling glass and uneven black stones.

The following week you read in the papers that Secretary Hogarth has said that seamen can take jobs to keep the strike going. You go into the union, and they say it's a tactic to hold out longer. Many are on their bones now, especially with the docking of the early ships and the strike fund is running low. You see Eddy again and Paddy Hayes whose cousin is a ganger on the buildings, and they are going to try for that game and by the end of the week the three of them are taken on and winding their way out of town on the works' bus; gazing out the window at the passing pieces of countryside and the blackened bricks of old churches standing in villages beyond Sefton and the hell of a difference between that and the quiet docks.

Each Friday they go down to the union and sign the register and put their strike pay in the contributions box, and there's talk of a good many others doing the same. The blocker behind the desk asks how's it going, and they have a laugh and say.

'Alright.'

Then pick up the boards and stand on the dockside for a day. Come the Monday they'd be in the country again and changed work clothes for the pick and shovel and the days pass slowly and the sun shines and dinner times they sit and play cards or boot the ball about in great, scrappy football games on a sandy field levelled by the bulldozers used for clearing the rubble as the huge estate grows up around their ears.

The feeling is stronger as they go through June. Few ships are docking now and there are hundreds more strung side by side out from the quays. And the feeling stays in the walk down the stones and passed the quiet offices and ships hovering above the walls; idle and empty as much like iron ghosts without men to work them and the little clutches of people at the gates; no creak of winches or derricks swinging back and forth to disturb the sun on the water or pull out cargo from the long sheds, their tarred roofs wilting and hazing in the heat.

They ride the works' bus each morning and look out as the city gives way to the fields. And one day in late June, with the strike nearly seven weeks old, Jackie opens the paper and there on the headlines in big black type are the lines about Communists and the Seamen, and underneath what Premier Wilson has to say about a tight-knit group of men holding democracy to hostage. And you find Eddy and ask what's going on and Eddy shakes his head and shrugs. And Paddy Hayes who has been fighting again says it's all a load of shite. Fighting again, in the great shines and lumps about his face, and he says 'Shite' to everything that gets on his nerves. He used to live near the old house; his home like a bomb shelter with his old man raging. They were known as fighters all around our part of the city. He loved our auntie. She's looked after him many a time when he had nowhere else to go. You smoke and look out of the window.

They go back to work and everyone is talking about it; the moaners making a meal and even the good ones not saying much. The crawlers laugh sarcastically about whip-rounds just to support the commo's and who wants to have them buggers here anyway; all they want is to wreck the country with their bloody meetings, screaming and bawling for all the workers to join together, when there'd be no work for anyone.

And all day long, it's Communist this and Communist that. Jackie looks over the hut and there is Eddy with his face in the paper not saying much, so Paddy stands up and shouts at the ones doing all the crying; Eddy looks up next and one of them turns to him quick as he's on his way out.

'Why don't you go back to Russia,' he shouts.

And there is damn near a fight. The ganger comes in, and even if he is Paddy's cousin, he doesn't look too pleased. It's the same on the picket line. People are shouting at you down from the buses and you couldn't remember that before and you could swear you heard that word Communist more times in the next few days than you have ever done in your life. They tell Eddy where to go, like he's a bloody Tink himself, and now you listen to them moan in the workshops and on the docks. It makes you wonder, with Nelly Flanagan giving you a free drink now and then and Joey Maguire on the buses and the occasional whip-rounds for the poor, who are these bastard Commos?

It is even worse on Sunday, with the papers full of the story, and one even has a special centre page spread devoted to the strike with pictures of the seaman's executive lined up, side by side in little boxes until they filled the two pages like mug shots of convicts. The ones supposed to be communists or sympathisers are circled with a big black ring. There are even pictures of Secretary Hogarth, but he isn't saying anything; the bastard and a couple of boys say he's always wanted us back after that Pearson report. All that week he's on the television and the wireless and you can see he isn't scared any more, and everyone is nice and respectful to him, and even looks like they feel sorry for him having to deal with those traitors in the union.

Then you're humping timber and laying out roof joists and making ready for the joiners when one of the moaners passes by and he's laughing and makes a sign to pick up your cards,

'Nine, ten, jack mate, off you go, fucken back.'

Shouts over that the strike has been cancelled. You find the others and take an early bus home to catch the news and your old lady gives Eddy some tea, and your old man is sat in the chair and Hogarth comes on and he's looking serious, with his little face and eyes peering over his glasses and that faint Scottish accent and says the executives have taken a decision to end the dispute.

And no-one asks him what makes the seamen change their minds so sudden before he drones on about the Prime Minister's speech and how talk of Communism does not affect in any way the executives' decision. The old man starts to laugh. And you don't know what to think and sit looking at the bastard and wonder about all the good lads who have watched the days and weeks go by with fluff in their pockets, and you look over at Eddy and he says nothing. Then your old man says that they're all the bloody same anyway.

So, you go back. It is as simple as that. And oh, they are as nice as pie to you down the 'Pool; mister this and mister that and would you like to come this way. That would change soon enough when they had their ships away. You feel lousy as you ride down on the bus to the Harrison yards and Barney Hayes says 'Forget it, you'll be sailing out before the end of the week,' so you look around you and try hard not to bother.

That night after they sign the book they go down the pub and drink pint after pint, and Eddy starts on again about his freedom and Paddy tells him to give it a miss; it's all over now isn't it ?

'It's all shite.'

And they take a taxi up to the South end and give Nelly Flanagan a few bob back for all her good turns. And woman that she is, she buys them a few off the top shelf herself and the rum and the whisky is still going down when she closes up and draws the curtains in a way only the untouchables understand.

They drink some more until there are only shillings left from the advance notes then go whirling down past the dock walls and even at this time you can see ships lights moving through the locks to the half tide basins and hear the tugs rumbling across the water. They fall laughing up the gangplank and an officer looks down from the bridge and gives a sad little smile. Paddy hammers his feet against the steel and shouts.

'Don't laugh at us, you cunt.'

He kicks a cardboard box that goes spinning through the night and lands on the water below, the brown oily water unruffled by ships these past seven weeks and which welcomes all fighters.

'I try not to be bitter son, but the priests and the whisky have me helpless.' Our auntie blows her nose like the wind in a sail. She points to her lover stood by the big black car with its whitewall tyres that had already seen trips to Spain and Rome with another man, her husband. He scuffs his shoes and fiddles, a man gone wrong, nineteen years younger, adrift amidst her hopeless visions.

'He dredges me,' she says.

On the deck the middle of the morning, the sun sprinkles the water and glistens on the winches and loading booms with the Mates nice as pie and Jackie standing there, not doing much and no-one seeming to care, and engineers coming up from below tell you how much they have enjoyed the rest and the subsistence money and have we had a nice holiday. They stop clowning when they see Eddy's face.

The third Mate comes up and tells you a bit curt to do something, and the Chief catches hold of him and weaves him down the companionway and pulls him to one side, and everyone can see he's putting a fly in his ear.

The Dockers are just coming back from the welt and there's a few lads hanging around the galley to see what's on for dinner and the winches haven't started up again yet and suddenly, there's a moment of great quietness on the dock, with the ships resting in the haze and a faint drone of the city beyond and the smell of tarpaulin and oil mixing in the warm air. You hear Eddy's voice mumbling something and it grows louder, and you look up and see him there with the hair down one side of his face as he flings aside the painting rag and pushes his hand up and your mind goes racing to the time when he sang 'The Saints' out on the deck so long ago.

And he's cursing the mates and the engineers and the owners and every bastard, on again about wasted lives and what it does; and a couple of the lads start smiling and this sets him off worse, and you stand there looking at him and think of all the times you've spent together, the hanging round and the waiting down on the docks, the building sites and the laughs, then the union's sad voice telling us to go back.

Well, we are back, back in the same old game and sailing on the night tide and it rises up inside you and Eddy's working his tongue around Communism and roaring it out till it rings down the stones. People are looking now. The moment of quietness has passed, and Eddy stands within it and the words; torrents of them float down the water and the Bosun comes up to get a grip of him but he's having none of it. You can see the skipper peering down from the bridge and you don't care, because no bastards can sail the ships without us, and you listen hard as he curses and shouts Communism back in their faces and watches them blink.

And it's a sunny morning in Liverpool and the strike is finished, but the voice won't go away, and things are never the same. Then when Eddy has said his piece, you make a smoke for him and go back to work and no one says a word and you turn to see the deck is deserted and Barney Conlan looks over and smiles and so does Eddy, as if he's just returned from the dead.

THE EXPLORER

Another Harrison ship that ran between Liverpool and the West Indies.
A real sugar and rum boat. John Paul joined her in Liverpool immediately
after the Seaman's Strike of 1966.

Thirteen

We are born and then we go away again. Things are going to change all right, and things are going to be different, but Jackie doesn't know if it matters much out of the Irish Sea. You had a go, that's all. It is in the afterwards that the forgetting becomes an art: the West Indies again on smooth running ships and Barbados and Saint Kitts and Saint Lucia settling into daytimes where mornings are spent working and the yellow afternoons left waiting for a drink. The talk carries change within it but time and distance all play a part and you can never figure out the in between times when you go away or when you are home. Time and distance, they have won a few things but the rules remain unbroken and the old know the way things blow; mountains of talk, always mountains of talk whenever there is a wind of change but for the gone men of the cargo boats what does it mean?

The lad with ginger hair from Birkenhead dances with a rose in his teeth a drunken pirouette across the pantry floor. A few of the deck crowd break open the bond. An engineer goes mad and tries to throw himself over; things are settling down. The opposition is happy. The skipper has talks with his engineer and mate; juniors would be brought up to enquire about the feelings of the crew. The sun is a blessing, the run not hard and everyone glad to be back at work. These are the messages they return with and the truth is not so different. Only the few mutter in their cabins about constant pressure and together the talk ends in building a proper democratic union.

The way it ended murders any hope for more. Yet strange within this is the talk of the old who have seen worse, experienced the betrayals, been hunted for their loyalty, told to keep going, and keep their own counsel. The young have only the feelings of betrayal, the hurt and the fleeting moments of glory; the old, called upon to bandage the sores, produce their solace in galleys or on deck, based in a language outside all the coded boundaries and united comfort of good drink. But the young are always the young in these things and you team up with those who regularly sing and you only learn over the trips with the crack and the jangle of what has gone before you.

'Where are we going Jackie? 'She used to ask.

'Are we stupid. What do we dream about when we dream about love?'

Then she would sing in her hoarse whisky voice,

'When the wind blows cold, d'you think about love.
When you see me lover, what do you see?'

You hear The Aunties song repeated over and over
again,

'Can you see me Lover, lover is it me?'

'There'd be days boy,' you'd be told in voices that bring
back wild times around the Cape or slumbering would
burst into madness and locked within it, the fight
for the union and behind that, the money needed to
live. Days, years back in the general strike when the
local union gets the call in Liverpool, and some of the
Catholics say they have no right to have them come
out but they always say that, strung out on God and
all the port idle but the local leaders get tossed aside
and the Marine Workers Union say we want a voice
and the Maritime Board council say ' no; renegade
communists bastards here,' even though they have
twenty-five thousand supporters in Liverpool and
other major ports.

'No-one is allowed to talk for the seamen except us
'The official Union says.

Forty years have passed but the old talk about it like yesterday, the lost nine days and the owners sit back, and the established union sits on its hands and between them wait until the smoke has cleared and the stage set for when no seaman can sail without their permission and the union's stamp. The first closed shop in the world and like most of them it saves everyone a lot of trouble.

'Everything else got smashed;' one of the Mahoney brother's is talking.

'Smashed like all the others. Men or opposition, funds from the old marine union still at Companies House, or where the fuck they keep the things: Untouched, that was where Joe Cotter earned his few bob, telling tales on his old friends. The quisling Cotter.'

'Only one union in this town.'

'For years we floundered son. We jumped ship or we backed out of things we had once fought for together. Many thought it's not worth the carrot and you just try to forget about things or make out alone. Terrible days son, terrible days. Fight back and you put yourself out of work when there was no work, stick on in and you become a 'company's man.' Any steady number and the union play your tune. What did we do kid? What could we do? Union as bad as the company and you needed your card; you had to live.'

One time Jackie is out on the hatch-tops in Latin America, miles up the Catatumbo river from Maraca-ibo and its night-time. The stars are out, purple and silver between the jungle and the lakes and the tales come bursting out again about the year the Irish boats got stopped and how the Irish Union was formed within De Valera's blockade, and how it became even more of a gangster Catholic outfit after the Liverpool men had brought it into being.

'Up on this same river with the *Mahia* that year; com-panies' boats used to run together on the river those days, one going up, one coming down. Sometimes they'd stop and do repairs. The *Buffalo*, coming up. Ever since she'd berthed, we heard tales of the Bosun. Big burly bastard from Bolton, driving them all hard and them having to take it, the times so tough. One lad, a junior ordinary seaman from the Dingle, he sets aside. Puts it about the kid is bent and wants him watched. He pressures this poor bastard day and night driving and working him, taunting him, whispering to him, an evil bastard. Then he brings out paper and says he's going to send a letter home to his parents and makes a show to get the crowd to sign it; some even did, they were that scared. The lad comes from a big waterfront family in that part of the city and he's terribly ashamed. The Bosun has him rattled and smiles and laughs and works him through murder in this heat and waves the letter in his face at night. One bastard. We heard tales of him all along that river.'

You think of Harry the Horse and that first lonely trip.

Frankie Boyle knocks his pipe out on the rail and the ash spills out in a shower of blue dust to the water below. Mahoney continues.

'Terrible heat, six days without air, we've come to berth alongside on our way down when one morning the watch goes to shake the kid's door and finds him hanging from a hook on the bulkhead with his tongue out and his face black with a yellow rope cutting into his neck. And what's worse, they hold an Officers inquiry up there on the Bridge and take no account of what the down-below crowd have to say. The Bosun has burned the letter and he's held free of all blame. But one of the crew holds up the burnt piece of paper he's retrieved from the ashes.'

'You let him continue sailing with us and we'll burn him,' he says.

'We'll do for him if he sails one day on this ship.'

Hard times or not, jobs or not, that Bosun won't make it back to Liverpool, not on that ship.

Mahoney waves out his hand to encompass the other riverbank.

'So, they ask our Skipper if we'll take the bastard back home. And the Captain says 'Certainly,' the way they all do when they're together, the 'gobshites.' They prepare to have him come aboard when the crowd here has their own jangle and Billy Evans says no ship is going to move from that quay with a murderer aboard.'

'Imagine what that took in the 1930's?'

'And when we get home, both the *Mahia* and the *Buffalo*, the company has the prosecutions all ready and asks the Union to be present. And in a Liverpool court Billy Evans gets nine months and twenty others are given a month apiece all at hard labour in Walton Jail. 'And you just know when the judge clears his throat and says?' and the usual silence that follows to let him have his line. 'Disobedience goes to the root of all things at sea,' and the union, the fucking union, half of them haven't been deep sea, stands there with the shipowner and say, 'Yes sir.'

The Horse comes into your mind again but you stay quiet as the skies change from velvet blue to the ashen sober skies of November and the coast comes in sight and so it goes with trips and day-times and night-times and sometimes bored and sometimes singing with a belly full and other days skinned out but talking, always the talking, in cabins, on deck-sides, in bars, in evenings, with broken sunlight across the waters, or in cold, washed-down galleys on the Irish Sea ,corner houses of the dock road; it falls all over you like a blanket spread across the Ocean pulled across endless days of sleeping weather, anticipation or depression dependent on which way the ship turns; in between times talk of fire and burning, bringing its own moments in all the rhythm of going away, 'till you don't know if you're a rebel or a sucker.

Seamen adrift and on the beach in the Northern States, picking apples in the blossom of Vermont or down on the coast and the lake ports of the St Lawrence seaway. On the docks through the Montreal Winters or ship repairs on pier sixty in New York, snow on the pavements and coffee in the air. And lives go by, much of it washed with wine and beer but most of it sober after the early festivals of backing out. Bums on the loose, all authorities and representatives would have you believe but now it's different, very different when the tales come from Conlan and others of sailing to the Argentine, or ending up on quaysides and flophouses through the murderous Chilean summers, change?

'What about the committees we ask for? What about the delegates from ships themselves instead of the carve-up at the big house? That's what the war done sonny. Said we were never going back.1947, a bad Winter in Liverpool; snow everywhere. People wouldn't take less, wanted more; more housing, more jobs, but they said our freedom was illusory.' We said, 'fuck the Owners, they can pay. We lost 30,000 seamen across the Atlantic.'

'They want us back and Yates had just become sec-retary and says, 'he doesn't want no trouble, neither from the shipowners nor the men.' And they have us back. It takes time but they had us and Barney Flynn and Billy Hart go to jail and Pat Murphy follows them and they say the union man Percy Knight is in tears in the Liverpool Sessions House, but it still did no good. They still lock us up. Hatred. Our boys, all the way from the 'Thirties to the Second World War, and where does it end ? but fighters boy, we had the fighters here and we've them to thank when we sit at good tables and sleep and eat clean; otherwise we go away and are forgotten.'

Jackie remembers his old man's talk of the night watchmen and their visions and there's no shortage of ships after the strike. Those few months you couldn't be home or away again faster. Debts are repaid and the barometer rises and just you try to get anyone to come out again in this climate. And in return there is the quiet campaign of change, but it has shifted from the deck back to the union house in London just like the old ones said it would and is issued in statements of members passing through the doors that have been opened to them but is a far cry from Eddy's shouting and the bitter chants of his mad song.

Change just the same, and it cannot be denied that there is a proudness of having stuck by the union and not being split the way they used to by everyone else but the rhythm of being back is lapping against resistance and it gets you on trips through the Leeward and Cape Vincent Islands when you are as quiet as the rest of them and wonder what it is all about.

You want to be a rebel and say fuck them all but how much of one are you inside? Being there with Eddy was all too pat, too easy and although you stood in the mud, there's more, much more you could have done. The coming away again is too easy; blues of those early trips mornings just as easily forgotten. You know that five years on the cargo carries no particular luck, not that it does in anything and maybe all the jangling has given you a history but one you don't know what to do with , not deep inside, more of an illusion really. of ease and laughter and good luck and good health and getting through the days amidst the lives and wreckage of older disappointed men.

Mexico is what you live for; that same history thousands have fought over, from bars and bodegas and backing out of ships the world over. The rain becomes heavier and pours in sheets down the windows. From a bar in Seaforth, you sit in a corner and look out at the silver Atlantic sky. Talk bubbles up around you and claims you as it always does and you respond and laugh. You are not a stranger even if fire plays a big part in the lovely in between world of the cargo boats but you want something more, some spark of what Eddy had inside him but not just the same.

'Sometimes there are stories we can never tell, too many bright colours, not enough paint.'

Jackie hears The Auntie's voice.

She is sitting by the fire; her hands shaking around the soup the old lady has brought her; the soup her own Da has distributed when the seamen were on the stones so many years before Jackie was even born.

'A man from the North Wall of Dublin; the Liberties,' she says proudly.

'Except he was not our Da; sometimes all we can do is throw our families to the wind.'

She shudders. You never knew what she means. The wind she always hated.

Fourteen

Time spent at home; nowhere better than the Liverpool docks, lines of warehouses and workers every morning, testimony to the exchange of goods and sounds of the banter coming from downtown to cross the world. The in-between world of night-time and days coming home, going away again that informs anyone from this city of tides and adoptees. You hang around the yards and the Harrison berths treading softly down to afternoon alehouses and timber and grain quaysides, kicking orange peel and crusts from rusted crane tracks into the black water, working with the docking gang from ship to company ship around the Canada and Alexandra and Gladstone docks; weekly wages instead of pay-off's; a steady a time of being on quayside after quayside on the purple river, feeling the wind that our Auntie hated blow around you; a wind you grow up with here.

The shore gang different; full of laughs and desperate jokes and dockers, thousands of them, carrying folded raincoats over the outstretched arms and the white mufflers of the old; dignity and respect down the generations to the young with short hair and shiny suits and going to town with big rings on their fingers as they sing their own song. So Catholic on this North end they pay them church attendance in 'the sweet six' golden hours of Sunday. Liverpool always the Queen of overtime ports where the bonus is paid on the tide but it's changing now and Protestants don't throw hammers anymore and left footers don't just follow Everton and the laughter stretches all the way wherever there is the work and anyone can take the corners without the old jokes, Billy Liddell, Jimmy Fell.

Going to the match with Bobby Jones; walking up the little side-streets off Fountains Road, dark in the night now with the drizzle of rain and pearl drops glistening on the porches, slippery underfoot and following in the wake of a thousand footsteps on the black pavements through otherwise quiet city streets to the park. The football ground and loyalties Jackie has grown up with through fathers and uncles and the Everton blue of the O'Neil's , Farrells and Donovan's and Eglington's; stories at Christmas through the haze of smoke and liquor, the glorious days at Goodison Park and that history means not a thing when you first stand on the empty terraced slopes of the Kop at a reserve team game and swing on the red rusty safety bars and know this will be your home forever.

And Bobby Jones tells of his first-time comings to Birkenhead, the one-eyed city, how scary it was after the quiet Llyn peninsula, alehouses and docks, broken by quaysides and huge floats, the slaughterhouse smell, smoke everywhere separated by penny bridges, funnels and roaring laughter. Coming in on a bus and leaving the green country lanes and dark certain mountains, he stands still and alone, gazing across the water to Liverpool, smoke rising everywhere as if from a giant furnace. Bobby's first time away from unemployed streets in Pwllheli and sees his first big Blue Funnel boat inching her way up the huge float to its berth and knowing it is for him to join amid the mills and tanneries and yellow sulphonic air dancing about him; the back-end of bombed-out and disused warehouses and blasting workshops of the waterfront against all the stately movement of the ship across the black water and he knows exactly why he came even though like you he is frightened. The misery of cold March, with grey clouds and spray coming up off the river, and the only thing that holds him in that first strange uncertain week is the trip to Liverpool for the match and the knowing soon he'd be on his way out to the Pacific.

Liverpool, Bobby's home now, staying with old auntie's whose ancestors the Thomas Jones built the once sedate streets around Princess Park. No pubs for a mile or more, where thousands of them prayed in huge Congregational churches called Bethels and lived and prospered, left legacies and went back home leaving only their most skilled to remain. Far away now from his quiet hillsides and villages where anyone has to leave for work and not always dream of going back but talk instead of the Blue Funnel line, the Welsh Marine and snow on the bridges of Kobe or over the Muko river and cherry blossom and warm bars and women.

All around them now the roar as the ground explodes and echoes down the terraces as the teams prance out of the tunnel into the glare of lights. And down dark streets later with pints and cigarettes and laughter they talk of the Crack of being home with the football and the ale and the weekends coming up in winter and spring. Nothing so sweet as being at home and knowing you can go away again, Liverpool the elsewhere city; you're starting to get it now.

It dances within you; makes you bold. Alone on a Saturday night in the club with the drink and music and She's there with her long black silk dress and hair flowing down to her shoulders. Her old man owns a dairy but she's an actress; dancing with her friends.

She laughs at his insolence as he barges in, affronted at first by his stage bravery but as time goes on and the friends leave, the music slows for the last numbers and her head is on your shoulder and her hands glide your back. Out, out into the night air with the breeze coming up from the shore they walk the coast road where the stars make winter patterns across the sky and teardrops hang off the trees. Over to the mate's house where his parents bed down early and you pray the living room will be free.

Your own tiny flat out of bounds now, the legacy of the fire, where the old lady and the old man and sister sleep cramped in the top rooms. No chance of going back there, the resurrection of the burning within us all. You say a silent prayer they're asleep. Quiet by the canal and the lighted yards; the smells of the night mix with alcohol and her perfume; holding and persuading and her quiet laughter as she hitches the silky dress up and climbs ahead of you through the downstairs window.

It remains quiet. No sounds come and first on the couch and then on the floor they bring cushions for support, and she stoops to bring down her underwear from beneath the shimmering dress, her platinum hair caught for one magic moment in the yellow gleam from the lamp outside. And quiet, so quiet, with everybody sleeping around them they make love, then doze; then fiercer with their mouths locked into shoulders they fuck into the floor and sleep until the light comes up in the sky outside and they hear coughing come from the next room and a quiet chuckle and wonder did his parents know everything all along?

Later, the smiling train to the quiet docks, the Bank Hall station, and disused lines glow with a shimmer of their own as the shadows of the early hour cling to them. Past the sleeping terraces painted in whites and reds and blues and the luminous river flowing away as it shapes and changes as much as the city itself and across the water the shipyard workers' homes clinging together in the early yellow light. She hails a lonely taxi and blows you a kiss goodbye.

Down to breakfast: just you and Bobby Jones; little work on Sunday; first shift all finished by eight o'clock and an hour or two down in the cabin with a mug of tea and time to work their own rhythm with the thought of her, the papers, the horses, the dogs and the football. No one to bother in those early hours before the shore gang comes aboard. So, turn up the radio, roll a smoke, grow dizzy and dream. The sight of her each time they play *Penny Lane*, gathering her shiny dress and beautiful long-limbed climb through the window; the shine of her hair, the smell of her perfume, and the ale in the pub at lunchtime has never tasted so sweet nor tobacco so good amid all the Sunday songs of the midday dock road.

Leaving the river those dreams are stilled when they head from the Mersey to the Clyde. The late afternoon, the hulks of new ships and yards in disrepair and the falling brickwork of the blackened tenements another reality after a night at sea. And Glasgow, poor sweet, devastated Glasgow with the evening sun and red sky over the rooftops mixing with the dusk to illuminate a city like it has been caught in the flames of some hell. Its heart being torn away and left staggering alone while the old ghettos are transported to the outskirts and the new ones await to take up the threads of yesterday's dream.

The lash of the new in the concrete high rises with nothing of the style of the prewar tenements and you don't need telling by the little feller who turns to them on the bus and says.

'This place is fucked son.'

Just the way they do in Liverpool. The shouting bus to the quiet dock on plantation quay that puts the auld one down by his street and he staggers away over the cobblestones, passed the disused barrows to where his isolated home still stands like a gallows in the shadows, lit like a lantern amidst the dark bricks and gable walls that leans towards the water and the black and silent cranes.

'What the fuck you are moaning about,' someone says. 'Youse never had to live down here.'

'There's got to be something better than this, just knocking everything down.'

'Better get back to your girl Sonny, before it's too late.' He's right. It is too late. The snow arrives next day with her letter but it's The Auntie talking.

'Jackie, the leaves, the trees, the river. The evening light on our Atlantic streets; this is what we call home son, more fantastic than any faraway place; here in our own beautiful city.'

The wind blows around her and bangs in the yard. You see her give a shudder and go inside to the fire.

'We're all from somewhere else son; all strangers to each other,' she whispers.

And it doesn't matter that the flakes gather along the railway tracks or that the engines lie waiting for their loads when you get down to Swansea; the lovely woman is gone. There are few lines to the letter. Snow covers the coal wagons in the railway yards, hurt sad, upset, it doesn't matter, you shout the odds instead; louder, if need be, the way every 'Dear John' is posted on the mess deck, pantry or saloon where laughter hides the fear, the fear of anyone who goes away and can't be seen to appear lost and alone, just one of those things.

Back in Liverpool you go downtown instead of meeting her. Try the *Queens* and *The Mona* and then up to *Ma Egerton's* then onto the wine-houses of Great Charlotte and Tarleton Streets, where you told them all you drank wine and they told you to shut it, 'wait till you've done a trip you cunt,' until the floor starts to roll and dance beneath you in a stunted shambles and someone threatens to put a fist in your face; it is the late afternoon, with the dark coming down and someone else talks of clubs and you stagger up Tithebarn Street and see the flyovers taking shape, their steel ribs like skeletons in the dusk and what has been pulled down now lies in heaps of stone and rubble alongside the road as far as 'little Italy' and you feel something else has been pulled out of you as well but you're just another number caught up in the game, the same game as everyone around here.

Sober, you go to see a great auntie the sister of the Nana on his mother's side , who lives on Benedict Street up from Scotland Road and below them finds whole streets gone and the roads widened out and straightened where the houses used to be and remembers bus rides out from the city years before as a kid to Litherland and to Thornton and the bus inching along the same road and the houses and alleys and lanes pouring with people and carts and red wagons and now they have now cleared the fucken lot.

The great auntie in her black clothes and braided silver hair shows him pictures from back then with the same road full of courts and middens and ash pits everywhere and people starving if the ships didn't come and you think maybe it wasn't all that great then; maybe it was always fucked, a cracked swollen time with the people to match; a place of characters?

You need a change: to be on the move again. Cigarettes and papers; the wireless in the cabin; the walk down to the dock, the early paper clacking against your leg doesn't have the same ring about it after she's gone. The strike is long away now, and Eddy is in

Latin America and the Conlan's somewhere in the Med. Away, away, and you think why you don't get out under your own steam and fuck this game. Ships everywhere and that night they go to the alehouse and get told the *Canada* is due at the landing stage the following morning and they would be taking names for a quick turn- around to Montreal before the cruises would start from New York.

With a drink warming the blood and loosening the head, you tell Bobby you've had enough of the shore gang. The *Canada* is the big white ship and you have only worked the cargo; now you want away; *Penny Lane* only brings back memories.

'Stick around Bud. Hang around and we'll sail again with Harrisons.' Bobby says.

'Someone spoke for me,' you hold up your book to the official taking names.

'Done a trip have you La !!!' he spits.

Said in the way, the Lloyds List used to code their messages for those who waited on the docks. Then you see the line of smart-arses forming the queue at the landing stage and you're suddenly not so sure about leaving the Cargo. The river is misty grey and rolled flat in the drizzle and the great white Liner with her green funnel towers over the wooden stage and the ferry seems tiny as a bird as it comes breaking through the river from the Woodside terminal.

This crew men wear a different look about them with their snappy haircuts and smells of Cologne. Some of them arrive in cars and shake the keys and look around as if they have places to go. Their handle is an expensive look, mohair suits and cherry Como's or Brogues. Quieter than the mods in one way, louder than them in another with big sovereign rings and bracelets flashing as they scuffle their shoes and wait for their turn for when the emigration runs finish, and the big money starts on the cruises.

Cunard Yanks, even if they work the Canadian Pacific. The cutting for the number, the main chance, the heavy dollar: all etched out on faces as the bosses come down the plank and begin to sort the allocations, the same as in the dockers pen where the bum jobs all come out first and the same running and ducking and scuttling away and then, like bees around honey, the forest of hands when anything decent comes onto the slate. The cruises pay the dollars, but the crack that sparks the 'Cargo' is missing.

'This is nothin' pal, wait for the Bahamas when half of them will go missing.'

Pressure ; everything on the double and everything first-class; no poor émigrés now on the *Canada*, only 'punters' and 'players' and Jackie remembers Killer Baines telling him about the booming liner trade that sailed full to bursting between New York and Liverpool throughout the hungry 'thirties, when everyone else was starving or pinching a penny around here.

These stewards talk of *York* as if it's their hometown, New York and the Market Diner and Forty-Second Street and then out cruising around the Caribbean with Yankee bloods paying a dollar a day on the dropsy. Old timers who walk around like they are ships of state themselves, and have houses in the suburbs, clean their stained tuxedos with coffee and wait for the roll at the end of each cruise, hardly touch their wages, all their money sent home by allotment and never miss a trip where every new face is a threat; money stashed everywhere in secret places aboard.

Bedroom stewards, old arses hated by the young who want to move on up; everyone shifting and fighting and cutting for a piece of the action. American ways: American days, back home everything forgotten and they sway and roll and jaw with the best of them, in clubs or at lunchtime bars and back out again in the evening, sparkling white shirts under their overcoats on winter nights their faces buried into the collars shuffling along like James Dean with their *Judies*.

'When we were in Brooklyn.'

These guys for whom the biggest sin is not to hear them out or listen to their drawled stories, these Liverpool Yanks with their suits and coats and rings all forgotten in the sweatshops and cramped quarters the struggling and the cutting and the whipping of what goes down in the months away and what they have to do for a dollar; nothing matters now except to give them an ear and note their look; propping up the bar, Lime Street, Legs of Man, Friday nights.

'When we were in Maxi's, The Market Diner, 52nd Street.'

First days away, you see a lad from a MacAndrews' boat; Tommy MacNally, over a year now sailing the big ones and he's caught the same bug except it's the other way around. No talk of New York and Montreal and the big sunshine cruises, or what he's doing now, but when he was back on the cargo and calling at small bars, the crack in Pizza houses and cafes outside the docks in Genoa or Livorno where the huers build bonfires on the pavements and winter is frosted and red lit and cold and you could feel it real in those small bars instead of all this razzamatazz.

'You feel nothing here Jackie,' he says. And there it is again, the same old trouble; always wanting to be somewhere else. Liverpool, the place of somewhere else.

In Montreal you stay with MacNally down on the river and miss out the big spots on the main drag and in the afternoons end up where the French Dockers have their hiring hall, drinking coffee and brandy in an oven of a bar next door. Outside, the snow is piled up against the side-walks, and the sky is blue and shot with neon lights and raggedy wires for the trolley cars that run down to the water and they laugh at the poseurs on their way back from the cinemas and malls and jewelry shops of Saint Catherine Street.

'The fucken Atlantic roll on them,' MacNally sneers.

The thought of a six-month cruise on this madhouse finishes you; the Yanks driving everyone crazy with their steak and shrimps for breakfast. White-coated wingers drenched in sweat before the first sitting and the second sitters baying and howling to be let in the saloon. Crack-up's. Who will go on the bottle first in great sweeping sessions and be thrown out of the gang; one hundred replacements waiting to step up. The employers know the pressure of these trips; the queues for breakfast and the cooks all cursing; the sun across the islands shimmering across the blue Caribbean; everywhere tranquil and just awaking when this lunatic asylum arrives, hooters blaring into harbours that once saw from their watchtowers other very different types of cargo. No thanks. You want out. Drive you crazy if you stay; take another drink and end up back in Liverpool and you think wouldn't it be great to be down in New Orleans and you know then you've got the same bug.

You see the town falling down and the pictures of the strike suddenly rush back clearer than ever, and they are ripping up Cleveland Square and the old union office and the Sailors Home on Canning Place and you grab a coffee on the corner of South John Street, where the brown polished bricks and marble columns still stand and bump into Paddy Bennett an old timer from year's back. And all he wants is to talk about the strike and the Labour Party and the Communist Party and how we have all been let down. Communism in Liverpool, fiddling with his glasses he ends up saying:

'Jackie, this used to be a good town once.'

There it is again, everyone talking about the time before. You'd have to run hard to catch the gone men here.

'And even then,' Paddy continues, 'the place was fucked.' And he laughs.

Laughs out loud so people taking an early coffee stop and stare. You laugh with him.

'You don't have to tell me that,' you say.

And suddenly in that moment everything becomes clear, and you realise it's not only a place you have to get away from but yourself, the feeling both inside and out, to make something happen without confining you to ships or bricks.

Fifteen

The in between world of where you're coming from and where you're going not only battered by ships has the idea beginning to form inside him: issued off his own streets to the great boulevards of the Americas and the messages the poor always carry like laughter on the lumpy concrete highways they have constructed around this city, he is sooner than expected back on the Cargo. The one experience of big ships behind you and the frozen early mornings after Christmas bring a great supply of them. No one wants to go away around the holidays but here's the chance of money on the Scandinavian run, in the shape of a Christian Salveson short sea coaster and a travel pass for North Wales the day after Saint Stephen's day where the ship needs a second cook who will also double up on the deck. You sign a new set of papers and receive your new designation, all in one go. Happy to be away in the drizzle and the mist.

The dock contains just this one tiny ship that claws to the quayside like a rusty crab, adorned with ropes and hawsers and tarpaulins on the deck, red lead glistening under the rain; the accommodation sheers up steep and hatches are open that unload timber alongside the steel wires and battered covers that snake towards the sodden wooden gangway.

'Glad you could come,' says the cook.

'Away hame a day or two, there no bad here,' and he nods to where men plod up the deck or look inside to see what's happening or inquire in soft musical voices about the time, code for what's cooking.

'All Shetlanders.' He pauses. 'Don't cross them.'

He touches his finger to his nose.

The chief engineer wanders in, a huge bloated man with teeth like bombed houses and a piece of cord holding up his trousers, he's left in command while the skipper goes up the road with the cook. Both of them carry extra bags. The Chief brings out the bottle and calls the crowd, lumbering around the stove with the glass twinkling, jerking up his trousers with his thumb and starts to sing a song in a cracked baritone, raising his mashed fingers to the air.

An old time whaling man like all of them here with this north of the border crew, who has served his time on the fishing boats out of Buckie, who saves his

money and gets his tickets and buys his old mother
a house by the harbour , never marries and when he
goes home ; never drinks, and instead walks miles
along cliff and rock and sails with the Shetlanders and
the Salveson Line and just goes crazy in port when
the ship stops its engines. A great man but like many
of them, a terror when drunk and not to be crossed.

'Blasted them with the harpoon gun sonny,' and the
Shetlanders are grinning now, in their mashed down
seaman's caps and heavy boots. The lights up high in
their eyes and drink running smooth within them that
makes up the best part of the ship.

Too late to do anything else, Jackie takes the best steak
brought aboard that morning. A gift from the Chandlers for the Captain's dropsy and only used for special
occasions; but fuck him, hasn't he gone back to Leith
with the cook; so you take the steak and cut it up in
fine slices; put spuds to boil and drag peas and green
beans out of tins; ice cream from cartons and works
in a frenzy setting it all out until the galley is full
of steam and smoke and sweat; Jackie known as the
worst cook in the world, but he dives below for dried
peppers and tinned pineapples with syrup and rustles
up a salad from leeks and red onions and boy have they
brought up some stuff from the village before they set

off. Maybe the Cook knows the score!!!

The crowd are peering in to see what's going on and see
you jumping like a dervish and hopping from block to
cooking block and the old stove belching and roaring
like a furnace. Afterward, the compliments flow heavy
as the drink and more than plenty is laid down before
you ; grub is everything in these strange post-Christ-
mas days where everywhere lies silent along the dock.

'Ye've fucked ma budget,' says the cook when he returns.

Fuck his budget. You take the consequences when
you leave the stove. The ship moves a cargo of slate
across the North Sea, then slow from Stavanger up
to Trondheim and after five days at sea with snow
falling on the quayside in the late afternoon, the lights
twinkle on the hillsides like silver toys. Scarce a soul
around, all snug and tucked away in their red timbered
homes and the night comes on with an emptiness that
is transformed with the stars. Trees sparkle in the
frozen night. Miles to walk along near Artic roads
and lanes cleared back from the snow before there is
a chance of drink. And Jackie and Frankie Gallagher,
the third engineer, from the Upper Clyde shipyards
walk out together, showered and sharp and sucking in
huge gobfulls of the night air that makes their faces

even redder, and Frankie blows it out in steam like a horse; his green and white Celtic scarf muffled around his throat. They stamp their feet on the packed snow as the occasional flakes from the trees flutter about them like winter butterflies.

Thirsty and warm, sparkling eyes and glowing cheeks later they see the lights. The place looks like a country and western motel as they walk into the wooden building beneath the reindeer horns and hear the music come lilting out of the jukebox. Sit at the bar and have a bit of the crack as the music turns louder and there's a smell of cigars and cigarettes mixed with sweat and coffee and yellow beer.

Once in a while a woman looks up, but mostly they just sit around and drink with fellers, in check shirts who all look as if they've come off the trucks that sweep by with huge ice chains wrapped around their wheels. And Frankie gets up and has a dance and twiddles around, but there's not much doing and after a bit comes to sit down again, and even more flushed and his hair wispy says '*Watch out.*' A big feller with his hair tied back is dancing with his wife and then comes over and snarls something at Frankie.

Frankie says, '*Sorry pal,*' and looks down at his glass.

The guy walks away and Frankie shrugs, then smiles. They were those sorts of nights; Norway was that sort of place.

A place that you could only wonder at between the world of fjords and small hamlets against the noisy windblown Caribbean. Cold quayside berths from Oslo to Iggesund and Knivesdal, Scandinavian certainties from the quiet Welsh coastline and yet you stay on the run all winter, the ship sheltering between Scottish Islands and across the North Sea with the bow pitching and snorting like a horse you wake from afternoon sleeps and see skies full of yellow and grey; then the sun, sunken and watery, transformed in sheets as the waves crash over the deck and run streaming against the portholes; the Shetlanders themselves who seem as if they have lived all their lives this way, rolling with the blow, balancing with the waves, soft laughter and always the gentle laughter from men who are as hard as nails.

Jackie looks out and sees Tommy McCafferty's old man in his mind's eye, who settles in Liverpool after years on the whaling and the millionaires nights ashore on Lime Street; caught out of his time with Mary Murphy and now lives far from these islands on a big estate in Kirkby, his tears and his lonely playing of a sad fiddle one New Year's Eve party.

Mary, dancing and laughing with their guests drinking and singing; shouts over,

'Wha' the fuck's wrong with him?'

The kids shaking their heads caught between laughing and crying know all the time what's wrong when he takes a drink?

The city is their home but for him it's somewhere *else*.

'He'll be alright in the morning,' Tommy says.

A time of false starts as spring comes near and the weather breaks and you no longer see chains on the big trucks nor the ice floes on the water or the brown logs encased in snow, static across the lake waiting to be transported. A time that neither passes nor goes forward but is rather held within itself; a quietness that is lived and breathed and people become knowing about the absences that govern their lives; then suddenly the light becomes clearer, the snows melt, rivers rush, the wood turns yellow, the sun becomes warmer, the days longer, the air more perfumed with flowers and they forget and start to dance. Winter is too much to face but is for another time and the ship is given orders with the wind and the sun across the water to go to Poland and load timber.

'And keep back a few bob,' Geordie says and fills the tiny glasses and ever mindful, you think what a fine crowd this is.

They hove-to in the south of Sweden and make down the blackness of the Kiel Canal and like smugglers you and the Cook peer out to the smudged landscape beyond; the sole stuttering light in the high bridge house like some old storm lamp in the crow's nest. The captain and the pilot turn into shadows during the long hours and emerge stubble-faced creatures with the dawn. You go aloft and bring mugs of tea as the drizzle falls with the early morning across the flat Polish countryside.

Midday they have docked and the guards with their polished buttons and guns are already posted alongside the quayside. The cook is doing good trade with the whisky he sells for the captain. Too busy to start with the dinner, Jackie ties ropes and finishes off in the galley and hears laughter bouncing down the alleyway from the room the cook uses as his office. Peering out you see him shaking hands and putting his arm around glazed looking harbour officials. The chief engineer, who doesn't know much about these things, except boilers, pistons engines and drinking is also being embraced amidst their tears. He has not drunk enough yet, he looks embarrassed. Good business here in Eastern Europe. No sooner down the plank and a van ride to the town than notes and bottles are exchanged quietly in a cafe that huddles in a green light behind net curtains and from which the driver has a message to take them nowhere else ; Eddy's Bar; pockets full of big notes, the port of Gdynia, they pile in, who needs food?

Men and women sit at little brown tables with pink-ribboned lights reading solemn newspapers. The women all look withdrawn and the crew are crestfallen, thinking they have been told wrong. You are about to leave, when Geordies steady hand is placed across you and bids you to stay as he serenely hands over his currency for change and has a bottle of cherry brandy beside him as he counts the returns and smokes, a cigarette hanging with a smile on his cracked face. From a corner three men are donning white waiter's jackets and then, as the closing bells ring gently around the room all goes quiet for an instant. Then a trapdoor opens in the middle of the wooden floor and from it emerges a Maître D dressed in evening suit, ruffed white shirt and full red bow tie who announces the opening of the cabaret, like it was something from the Jazz age. Behind him comes the sounds of swing where the musicians are striking their chords and as the occupants tumble down the stairs they beat out a tune that bounces off the walls and touches everyone with its joy, the fresh sounds of party, party, season's changing.

Down below are all the drinks you could not buy above. For beer you must also buy spirits. Jackie, with his pockets bulging from the rolls of Zloty's buys vodka and lager. A millionaire for the night that has been the ruin of so many others from the fly houses of Argentina to the whalers at the Yankee bar. You carry the stamp of every seafarer, food and drink and women, the seraphim of every night in port. Tables cluster together with their red checkered cloths and guttering candles. You stand at the edge of the dance floor, and as the combo blows away in a fury, drink in the sounds as they carry like oxygen to the famished brains of the crew.

Women who have sat reading the financial papers and sipping coffee are now dancing and twisting like snakes as the floor bends and sways to accommodate them. The skipper is away, closely followed by his lieutenant and treasurer, the fat cook; the vodka sits well on the brandy and is washed down in a torrent of pilsner. Suddenly, from across the room, there is a woman at Jackie's elbow, and Geordie regards you and raises his eyebrows as you approach the wooden floor and begin to dance. The night has a certain promise that flushes it warm and secure with the smell of hot food wafting across the floor through to the happy bodies swaying like the candle flames on the floor.

Your friend twice his age, but beautiful with her clothes and styled long hair, sits down and orders more vegetables, potatoes and meat and the bill becomes huge in the pink light, but are you worried; everything is for nothing here in the great exchange? And the cook, with his lady, tucks in as well, needing reinforcement for all the drink he has glugged and what more he needs to sell and the zithers are zinging and the place becomes as hot as a furnace with the smell of drink and sweat and heavy food followed by shouts and curses and the occasional dropping of plates or smash of glass followed by hysterical laughter. The waiters are knocking it back as much as the musicians and on and on it goes into the night, the walls heaving like drayhorses, a party for all the world.

Then, as suddenly as it begun, the music slows and fades and the Maître again makes an appearance to signify the close and couples begin to drift away and the dance floor becomes deserted, as if some magic order has been passed, for all the fun, all the happiness on earth to come to an end. It leaves behind a glittering mass of bottles and plates that shine like a sheet of stars across the empty tables.

Jackie sees his auntie's face and hears her say in her ruined drunken voice,

'This is my house. The others think they own it but it is mine. Your Nana always used to take soup with your Dada when they were on strike, a union man. They called him a communist, but he was only Saint Vincent De Paul, 'We'll be around a lot longer than the Commo's, he used to say.'

'Take my friends home in our taxi, 'Jackie's woman commands.

No problem, you agree flashing another note. Stuttering across the city, with the rain on the pavements and beating on the windows, they travel through quiet dark streets. When the car stops you pay the driver, and the woman takes your arm.

THE FIDRA

John Paul joined her 3 days before the New Year of 1968 at Mostyn Docks, North Wales; the only member of the crew from south of the border. An old whaling ship built in the early 1950's for the South Atlantic trade; her major cargo was taking granite and slate to Norway and other ports of Scandinavia and the Baltic. She carried such a good crew that John Paul and stayed on her for over 6 months, the longest he had been on any ship.

Suddenly the last one is gone, only a couple of Zloty coins jingle in your pocket. In a panicked fumble you search for the comfortable wad you carried earlier. No use, nothing there. They walk past a heavy wooden door and into a courtyard where she opens a smaller one and they go upstairs. A sea of dark mahogany drowns everything, the chair, the wardrobe, and the chest of drawers with a piece of red velvet that decorates the surface. It might have been smart before the war now it just looks like something from another age.

Her bedroom is the same; pieces of chintz and velvets of the same red empire curtains fall behind the dresser and over the windowsills. A green cover on the lamp dims the light and you watch her as she slowly undresses down to her underwear and climbs into bed. A smell of dampness and the rain-filled night outside suddenly seizes you and you hold onto her for warmth while she slowly strokes you and reaches out to bring down the darkness. The heat of Mexico is a long way away now, but the drink is settled, and the food has helped and they are able to fuck and come back for more after dozing and all absences laid aside, you lean into her again. Food and drink and women, the old dream of the famine parishes. She gasps until the calm eases both your jangled senses and you sleep like babies in the cold wet night with the bedclothes clamped around you like a glove.

In the dream She comes to him in the airless room, the way she sits on her lover. The room full of May and her bold but faded dresses and laughs her soft dancers laugh and spins you Jackie through her arms and smells of whisky. She lives in another house now after the fire. The room rented, the lover at church but no way would you escape her now. You are hers amidst her own visions and dreams. She says you love her, and she loves you and it is as simple as that when all you wants is to ask about the longing, the burning, the betrayal and she laughs again, and her smile lights up the room like a lantern.

The morning comes through the window in a tired grey cold. The dream stays alongside in a shadowy grip. You get up and puts on your clothes. There is no coffee. You have no money. She shrugs her shoulders, and anxious to present her with something you rip off your cotton shirt. She takes it with a smile but without any great enthusiasm; it's only a token but its clean and its nylon bright. She smiles again.

Out on the streets of Gdynia on a Saturday morning; *Cast in nothingness, friendless and solitary* no red check tablecloths or blue skies here, only the cold drizzle slanting down the square and the black barracks of tenement flats rising above them. You pull the overcoat tight; in your blue mohair suit you fasten the top buttons against the damp sea wind. Wandering into a bus queue you ask men and women the way to the docks. No one can help. Helplessness, like the dream, rides inside you and eyes turning from side to side you take in the long tram-lined avenues and the few black cars going about their business. Out of the rain a man with a trilby hat and briefcase takes you to a tram stop and pays your fare and says a few words in English, and you nod your thanks; just another kind soul, a guy going to his silent work giving someone a hand, a jazz man treating a lost seaman as they appear in visions before them like the old ship's watchmen in Liverpool.

You make it back aboard; the cook is still drunk with a white raincoat draped over the broad shoulders of his working gear and storms away down the road in his galley boots, the sleeves of the 'mac flying behind him like a swan's wings.

'Give them the gear,' he says over his shoulder and points to the stove; all thoughts of his budget now thrown to the wind.

And returns hours later, staggering and face bleeding

where he's opened his cheek while storming the barbed wire and telling tales of his lost girlfriend and climbing the high fences by the massive shipyards when he's missed the gate and the guards with their machine guns can only stand and laugh; now his cheek runs with blood and he babbles about this life being so wonderful and he could live forever on days and nights like these. You hear later that the woman has been asking for you down at the bar and you feel sad you haven't made more of an effort to get there but that feeling doesn't last; you'll never forget her.

Life for this north of the island Protestants is different. They can't forget quick enough. For the cook and those others who go adrift, they will have to pay for the calumny of their actions. The remorse takes a little time to creep around the system as the alcohol departs but the quiet sea and thrum of the engines eats into their soul, as surely as night eats into day and captures them within a trawlers net of their own silence. In the galley the cook spends hours cleaning every cranny of the stove as if to purge his soul and the captain has brought to his working desk a huge Bible. It sits there remorseless as he works.

But it is late Spring now, and even if the wind still bites and the sea runs in a funnel down the Pentland Firth there's nothing like seeing the mountains go by beneath the clearer skies and these bright Islands, like the Islanders themselves, black hulks in the winter through a haze of mist and ice and smashed rain lancing into the sea, now stand green and shining in the sunlight; guardians to a different world. You lie on the bunk and listen to the singsong voices that whisper down the alleyway in the middle of the night, the prayers and changing conversations of the watch, accustomed now to the boom and flutter of their songs, dream different ideas of where you might be in your own time, no matter how good the ship, getting away from the world of the cargo and dancing out on your own.

And one night in Sligo, the crossing from the Baltic, the North Sea and the blue Atlantic, quiet and calm in the evening light, you see the yellow and brown of the houses and the green shining turf banking the river and the timber wharf where it seems the whole village has come down to help clear the ship and you know what you've been thinking. The alleys lead away from the harbour to the town square , and the café lies open with its great ribbed steaks and a late sun comes pouring down and lays silken threads across the cornfields and you think about being away under your own steam instead of governed by the sound of running and bells and for the first time think about this place where you want to come back to from amongst the millions of the toiled and shifted poor; part of you belongs here in that curious world between home and away.

The illusions of the departed that you could come back here, away from your own city with its dirty laughing docksides and returning ships and clubs and yards with bricks shot through with sun amidst a tangle of television aerials and wires that buzz with song. Go back home. Say 'Hullo there ' and pack a bag for Dublin. Then you might walk the length of these fields in your time under your own steam in these fine serious days, like a man who has already been here and gone; like walking back to the past on the same road as the future; the gone man; there's the story.

Six weeks later, you stand high above the pier head on the topmost deck, the boat across the Irish Sea all salt and gulls and pass the sands at Seaforth where you learn to play football and down the channel where the river shines around you out to the calm water, late shadows, the sun lowering and above the funnel a gentle banked sky. Cigarette in hand, the Ferry has left the crowds that have come to see you off and you jangle with a lorry driver, all fair hair and oil ingrained hands. They take a drink together and see Irish girls wandering about and giggling and a few lads going home giving them the patter of any overnight boat. Come the morning they're in Dun Laoghaire harbour amidst the sound of ship horns and dockers waiting on the cobbles and you see them again with bites on their neck and wearing scarves and dark glasses, still laughing.

The driver is going to Kildare, you take the lift, but not before they have breakfast and eat bacon and eggs and sausages with big cups of tea by the wall before the Liffey awakens in front of their eyes. A fine blue mist with the sun on the rise and the bridges shaped like jumping hoops all along the North Wall as the river rides away to the Shannon, and you think what the Dada must have thought as he left the Liberties to go away forever.

The confidence of the young everywhere you hold out the thumb, dark glasses and a wry smile and before the sun goes down have passed through Clonmel and Bally Duff and over the knock-me-down mountains, and swept into Cork in the back of a farmer's old black and battered Mercedes. You see the ships lined up in the river, lying quiet with the sun fading on the paint and the rust and the quayside stone cracked and sprouting moss and the old yellow walls and a feeling in the air that reminds you of Sligo and the reasons why you came , all the more gentle and easy than those apprentice gangs roaring out their jokes with their football on Liverpool's cobbles; the way this old port has served Baltimore and New York in the same way as Naples has served Buenos Aires. Shipboard dreams.

You pick up the bag and take yourself out on the Kinsale Road and the weather is fine with tracings of white clouds that float like feathers over the sea. He hangs around in the sunshine and does not look at the map, but instead follows the road south bending by the water that takes him to Seven Head and Clonakilty Bay, and the country goes by and the sun burns and the boots begin to rub and that night he uses his bag for a pillow and stares out from beneath a window full of stars that gives out all over County Kerry.

A strange feeling as you walk around the shade-filled back streets lined with plane trees sloping to the fields and you enter once more into the dappled sun where the stones register the dead of the civil war, and the song of *San Francisco* spills out into the air and lights the water as if the country has been dredged. And yet behind this air of desolation there is a hum of life that bristles and sings and constantly aches for a way to express itself just like it does in Liverpool.

You stay in Skibbereen most of that day, walking slow

and purposeful around the town passed pastry shops and the diaries and cook a supper of sliced fried potatoes and eggs, tomatoes and cheese to follow and sit on the doorstep of the youth hostel. The place run by a big bustling woman who works and slogs and smokes her way through each day with a husband, who prefers to sit and drink tea and talk and by night play the fiddle for the amusement of the young as they happen by. Two Swedish girls come later, one with long blonde hair, the other dark and brown and not long afterwards the bottle is out and the instrument cuts and strums and zings deep into the late hours. The sisters grow tired, the wife is now tiredness personified showing in her face guides them to their bed and after they leave the fire goes out of the old man's playing.

At Baltimore the boat bobs at the quayside fresh from Clear Island and people are coming off and shaking hands and there are rolls of carpet and stores and great rusted cans of oil being stashed aboard and nets are rolled and bobbed with cork and oil-stained lumps of wood. The sun is shining in puddles where the tide has leaped the wall this morning, and groups of men stand and talk, flat caps and heavy brown shoes going back to the island, that shimmers off the coast like a vision of pearl above the haze of water, the last place in Ireland before the Western Ocean.

High above the harbour in the late sunshine you sit and gaze over the rough shale and blasted green hillside to the rocks and outer walls where the water jumps with mackerel and the great red mullet sweeps among them and the evening boat arrives complete with the sisters from Uppsala. Later they stand in the gathering cool of the quayside and tired and relaxed you put an arm around Katrina the blonde one's shoulders and she doesn't turn away, her hair billowing out on the wind.

Sunday you kneel in the church with the congregation sighing around him in Gaelic and the women dressed in black and the young with net veils and the men with those polished shoes that he's seen at Baltimore; interested only in the mass said in Gaelic not in the ceremony with its echoes of all those Sundays in Liverpool, Mass, Communion, Benediction long ago but Liverpool is not England; it is Philadelphia and New York and Chicago, Barranquilla and Baltimore, and even here on this island , the capital of inner and outer Liverpool shows itself, always a place somewhere beyond. You turn away from the plain wooden altar to look at the people and see amongst the clean-shave islanders one or two souls with bedraggled beards and fierce eyes staring back and when the priest has finished and the blessings served and the congregation satiated to move slowly from the church to the grassy

banks outside and stand talking in hushed tones, you
again encounter them.

'Come and have a drink man,' one of them says.

You walk back across a patch of field and another one
points over to the bar. Katrina is waiting for you on
the return, and she comes with you to the cliffs. The
clouds and the blue rain of the morning are blowing
away and the only sound is the roar of the wind as
they head up high over the water. The sun is trying
to break through and the stones on the headland are
slowly drying in the salt, the terns are calling and the
gulls crying, huge black headed gulls wheel and veer
as they reach the heights and you link an arm around
her and the warmth seeps up between you. Looking
for shelter they lie down in a hollow forged from the
rock and covered with the spring turf, and for what
seems like hours of rubbing and kissing you try and for
just as long she refuses, although in gestures accepts
you but with the protection of her clothes. Foiled upon
foil, Jackie failed Catholic and passionate, touchingly
erupts inside his kecks, and holds her with the wind
banging at his eardrums and the birds singing wild
above the water. You walk back dispirited and sunken
and sit sticky by the bar pouring down the Guinness,
while she takes whisky and smiles as the poets fly away

on their fiddles and smoke through broken teeth and nod sagely at her serenity.

The locals recount the happenings of home and abroad .The shaken head, the sipped pint, the pull on the Woodbine or the prosperous Sweet Afton. And at the mention of talk abroad more than one eye lights up among the travelers and the voices speak low of barricades and fire and the acrid smell of battle. And not just in France the voices murmur but in Germany too and Italy and the Ireland of the North but how they had to fight the Tans here and send them back to their English slums.

'Aye and raised the Tricolor over the Fastnet rock so we did, so we did,' another says delightedly.

Sunken in defeat you try to get something back and step in as though you have danced this tune before. On the docks when the seamen were striking and what you and the mates had done and what you hadn't and the great democratic spirit rising across the waterfront like Conlan was always on about between the ships the seamen, the union and the cause of Communism but really there was no more than bits of pieces picked up on deck and the usual banter of the lads who work the cargo.

Big evenings and days later, days full of pictures, with her blonde hair blowing wild and the clouds billowing up to ride hunchback on the sun, you are stood, waving in drink, like The Auntie of his dream on the hot streets of Dublin City, all smells of salt and cigars and tinkles of music and chimes of glasses. Karina is waving from afar and blows her kisses goodbye, she likes you she says, and Jackie, full of stories and songs takes the ferry back to Liverpool and wonders what the Shipping federation has down for him.

Good to be coming home; bowers of sunshine on the brown swirling river and the sun sits above the cranes where a yellow light trickles down over the shadows and rusted legs sit like spiders along the quays. Quiet on the docks in summer, the meat and timber trades fastened between the months of August and Spring, the fruit boats in September, holidays in the mill towns, the Liverpool slumber.

You watch the formation of the city take shape before you; its noises carrying images of places known as a kid, the blackened stone buildings moving out of tiny detail into a great rolling canvas as the ferry slides into the green of Princes dock and starts to berth across from Mann Island with the golden domes of the financial district shining down upon you.

'Scotland Road, Beatrice Street, Bedford Road, the Esplanade, Coronation Avenue, Edge moor Drive; the litany of happy houses where this family has its roots.' The old lady lays back in the chair, lazy cigarette in hand, most of her day done.

'Yes, and a family grave in the Ford cemetery, if we want it,' she adds. The old man nods his agreement, a Sunday dinner inside him.

'It was never your family,' she says.

Sixteen

You look around in the sunlight over to the Dispensary on the way down through Cleveland Square to the dock. dazed and confused, away in your own time but what does it mean in the land of ships and hooters and bells? Catch yourself on Jackie you hear a Shetland voice and strange you take a pint and wonder where the hell you've been with all the leave that was once in the pocket, gone now like the Zlotys in Gdynia and time hanging like a rag from a nail between you and the sea.

The clear sky and the breeze and the flats all down the South end blinding white and blowing with the thousand sheets hung out over tenement balconies. Below them carpets are beaten and flogged in a swarm of dust that flies out and settles on lorries as they rattle their way over the stones. By Wapping Rosie and Patsy sit in the Baltic Fleet and talk to the Norwegians, scuttled and club-less after their last big night and you remember Baltimore with a laugh and nights that have greatness stamped all over them; the crucifixions come later, fair winds to howling gales later, depending on what foot you kick with.

'And what persuasion would you be Jackie? The lilting laughter of the Shetlanders who don't worry about such things in others as in their own mortification; similar in its way to the Liverpool waterfront, the same ironic question on the docks.

'What school did you attend?'

Now in these fine summer days, life has a style of its own, gaggles of Dockers wait by the shed or others wander slowly through the gates; on the welt into the alehouse and passed the sleepy coasters; what does it have in store for you Jackie?

The sun is a powerful mixture of ignorance and hope; blonde in August and still through September and dying by early October before the rains come in November and you're offered a job as soon as you walk into the Pool. Like everything when you act like you don't care you get better than when you ask.

THE VILLEGAS

A MacAndrew's Line ship that traded in wine, fruit and general cargo between Liverpool and the Mediterranean , mainly Italy and Spain. These small ships painted green and white were much sought after in Liverpool because of the shortness of their voyages.

Bums on their way to the David Lewis, the ones not too far gone, hang around the bars and look at him with hope and a borrowed pint in their eyes. They want to show how they are still keeping sharp and, on the number, before you'd see them later, dazed, slugging wine with bombed out faces on the steps of Canning Place. You don't care, buy them all a pint; you've had a good time; pass a few bob over to a chorus of 'thanks mate'; visions of night-watchmen and the Da's words still there to remind you and Jackie no longer a tight arse but as generous as he always thought of himself to be.

It echoes in the letter that arrives for the Da one morning just before you were set to leave. Stamped from Formby further up the coast, a letter that says the sender is an old cousin many times removed who takes an interest in family history. And out of its cribbed lines and folded pages, spill names of Aunties and Nieces and Nephews and Cousins you'd never heard of; a whole gaggle of them from the time they all arrived at the Clarence dock from Cork and Dublin and Belfast and swelled still further the already swollen famine parishes.

Settled along the Liverpool river, they spill off the pages like shillings from the gas man , there are a few Catherine's and a couple of Mary's, one or two Patrick's and William's and Francis's, then their wives then their children, who married the Gilligan's, who then married the Flanagan's and the Smyths who came in and married the Wailey's and the circle turns again before it stops at your own tiny family. You'd have a job making sense of it all. It would need years. The ones who bore them but did not know them; the old man who thinks of himself an only child.

The letter is signed with love and *hope you enjoy* at the bottom, followed by two kisses, your cousin Jacky Farrell Dunn.

'Wow Da' you say, 'we have a big family.' Thinking of Harry the Horse who terrifies you into an isolation you think the situation doesn't warrant but stupidly does you a favour.

'Let's go and see them.'

'Most of them are dead,' the Da says and laughs.

'Come on Da,' you say.

'Too much water under the bridge son,' the Da says and laughs again but you cand see he's secretly pleased that someone has taken the trouble even if he's not going to do anything about it. Maybe it adds a gloss to his own trips over the water to County Down in the early days with our Ma.

'Go and get your gear.' He can see you are disappointed.

'They were before my time Jackie. My parents were good enough. If The Auntie had cracked on twenty years before she tried to burn us all out maybe it would have been different. It might have been different.'

'C'mon Da.'

'Too much time son, let them rest in peace, 'he says. 'We've had enough drama in this house.'

There it is again, fire the heart of all your longing but it's different now, you'd gone past it, a longing no longer. The Auntie has had her time. This McAndrews' boat is running around the coast of Spain, and you walk down to the Queens dock, hand in your discharge book and come away from the ship with a strange ease. You don't know what changes are taking place as they leave Liverpool in the evening of a summer drizzle and you can see the green hills from the banks that rise up on the peninsula and beyond the city the lights hazing on the purple dusk of the river but you have an idea.

Happy with the short run after the long jags but there is something else now. Three days later, after a smooth passage through the Bay they Hove to outside brown rainy Bilbao and drift into port along the river Nervion; see the old stone buildings and the green trees and the miles of grey factories and shipyards spread out below the hills and know that this is only the start. There are changes that lie before you, Ireland has shown you that and the drinks with short sleeved steel workers who all carry umbrellas in an air that smells wet and is soaked in cologne, sounds and smells of fish frying in the streets; the mountains of shells and seafood and the cool fresh perfume of the women in the mornings grip what you already know and leaves you knowing. All's that's missing is the detail. It places you where? Away from The Auntie, that's for sure.

The talk down below comes in bursts; a babble in a run so short that you hardly know where you are; like seamen the world over jangle of the endless ports on the Great Lakes or great rivers. Conversations cut short that has the ship tie up on more quaysides than Spanish holidays and on this Iberian coast always one or two of the older ones to talk about the place and stories they know from the time before, the same way every-one has to learn. Stories from Murcia to Cadiz and how the Braceros organised all across the Anarchist communes of Andalucía in those last months of the Republic before Franco's Army ripped everything away.

Freedom and absence, the old Libertarian dream and Guillermo and Juan exchange glances. Tired now, old FAI men, and still not able to go ashore onto their own home soil but instead watch the young soak up the wine and the women and not care or think of anything that goes before them or what they fought for all those years.

Three short trips to Spain that summer and Barcelona the heartland, the Vera Cruz you have only briefly witnessed and don't yet know. The gold-toothed man who sells a watch that breaks the first week; the bars and alleyways of the port that groan with Monkeys and smells of Africa; parrots and hashish in curtained backrooms, shouts and screams and palm trees that come from Cuba lining the dock road and the statue to Columbus, dancing amongst the smell of drains and heat and sun.

On your way down the coast again leaving the still waters of the inner quaysides, you see the ships line up along the great loading wharves and catch sight of a book by Ernest Hemingway lying on an engineer's bunk, *Death In The afternoon*. Borrow it and take it below and consume the yellowing pages with the sun hanging high over the sea and the light reflecting in from the porthole as if there was a white fire across the water; and suddenly the link between time and place and someone else writing about that place in your own time rings in your head; a vision revealed: Barcelona, his new Mexico.

Back in Liverpool, you leave the dock and go up past Chandlers and oily garages, butchers, tobacconists and marine fitters, past Chinatown's houses and the sounds of boots and metal clanging on the streets, where the old-timers hug their precious bottles out of sight of the police and where the bookshops are gathered on the corners to the right of the Bombed Out church and are painted red, yellow and blue like the way they are in Cartagena and the whole place smells of smoke and barbecued pork and you buy all the ones of Hemingway you can find.

On board you find out from other seamen that Jack Coward, the Communist, sailed on this same run thirty years before and brought copies of *The Communist Manifesto* hidden within the hard back covers of

Don Quixote.

'That's some going considering those times,' one of them says.

But you don't turn a hair let alone a page until the harbour comes up again at Bilbao and instead of strolling the Brownstone City and all the pockmarked rainbow of the evening paseo you pull up a stool on the back end of the deck and with a mixture of Guinness and Cider read quietly into the night, the magic sipping away with the stories and the drink beneath the arc lights and lapping water.

Juan the lamp-trimmer once a republican major who now lives in Liverpool spends his time painting vast pictures from the civil war that fill his cabin asks what you're reading.

'There's more to Spain than Fiesta,' he spits.

'That feller's a phony Jackie.' You laugh at the way he twists the Scouse with a Spanish accent.

Stops you later in the alleyway and hands you a book from his own collection. George Orwell's, *Homage to Catalunya*.

Nowhere like Barcelona from the moment of docking to the walk into the town, past the yellow sandstone tenements to the municipal buildings with the kids kicking the ball around in the square and massive Columbus pointing out over the sea and the smell of the filthy water and the days Summer heat that makes even the green trees droop with fatigue until the evening revives them, where the old sit on benches and the children skid and play and scrabble in the dust at their feet as they gaze for coolness to the sea, and the noise and shifting mass of the Ramblas rages unabated in waves right through the night, the drinking, the dancing, the quiet ones reading in dim lozenges of light that peer down from the darkened gothic buildings.

Great Barcelona; the washed blue shirt pulled over a pair of jeans and the wandering up the Ramblas swept and tossed and bobbed and smelling fresh from evening showers and the sea of people rushing towards the port out for the evening promenade below the overhanging plane trees and you feel the change, times and place and people. Bars where you drink too fast with excitement and get drunk too quickly on the whole vast sway of the canvas like one of Jose's mad paintings then the slow ramble down to the Barrio Chino and summer night-time smelling drains and alleys and the Calle San Pablo and steamy red-lit bars of Los Robadores, just off the corner where the whores, all sun-tanned from the beaches up the coast, come from France and Italy and as far away as Austria to work hard here and dance all summer.

And come on Jackie !!! You meet a lovely slim blonde woman from Marseille and have a drink with her in a bar with dark windows and coloured lights, she drinking only milk before they go through a street doorway upstairs to the honeycombed rooms that stretch down the alley and finish above a shop that sells herbs and coffee from varnished wooden counters and take off their clothes and lay sun-tanned on the white sheets while she, in her French style blows butterfly kisses around his balls then performed her speciality while he groans and comes up for the shudder and finishes minutes later, grasping and reaching as the flies dance under the electric light. In a strange way The Auntie is now more real to you than ever even if fire no longer scares you.

A wonderful woman, young and lithe who wants to save money for an easy winter and the expense of the skiing season, and you put your clothes on and ask if you can stay the night, then the shake of her head and the laughing smile. This isn't Vienna; the money is in the short timers and what about her sleep, she laughs again and what can you do but laugh with her, shrug and kiss her and go down again to the street and the square where there's a restaurant with chickens roasting outside on the spit and where you can have a glass of wine and bread with your wings and crisps, all for thirty pesetas and there's no better taste after a night out with a few beers and a blow through than to sit at the checkered oil cloth and eat and drink wine and watch the life go by and know you'd had some time.

Recovery in Valencia; recovery and recuperation in a warm bandaged breeze amongst the white buildings of the dockside and like her sipping milky coffee from under the awning of a dock cafe. It's as though you belong here, the phut phut of the scooters making their way from town to the beach, another Sunday, another berth. Relaxing and not spending money looking for women. And along the quays there is a quietness. Older men fish off the stones, sit on orange boxes in the sun and you go swimming with the young ones off the crew in the quiet waters of the late afternoon. Football on the television in the evening, sat next to people who wear heavy wrist-watches on brown arms and pocket-book wallets in their shirt top pockets; crowds more sedate here than Barcelona and dressed in yellow and black as the dusk comes down blue between courtyards and alleyways and the perfumed smell of flowers as darkness tumbles down.

The lights are being turned on across the harbour, Johnny Keogh has put on his dungarees and clean shirt and wanders across the bridge and the river to the old black church. And prays before the altar in the cool air, heavy with the smell of polished wood and baskets of herbs the women have left behind and the Eucharist in the gold chalice high above him, a supplicant to the torn feet of the suffering marble Christ who gazes down ; Johnny an older man now but still lean and fit and a long time fighter for the union in the days following the war.

He turns back to his Catholicism after years of looking away and is still not happy, with the wretched priests nor with the hidebound gospels but, older now, is searching for peace and finds it in prayer and communion of the old churches. And asks Jackie to come with him, spend some time alone with his thoughts instead of going to town but you won't have it, more of the time spent reading now in the quiet of the afternoon or the night and work is really something that only has to be done on the sea and there's little of that, the life of this coast and Liverpool where the ship is your only confinement.

'Come for a little peace before I kick the bucket son,'
he says.

Out of respect you walk with him across the bridge
to the far quays and wait under the awning of a bar
across from the flower adorned church and take a
sugared coffee and a single brandy even though you
shouldn't and watch people pass by and smoke until
Johnny returns in the lilac dusk, his face all calm and
placid. You fix an eye on ships in the dock, the days
in Ireland still within you and the chit chat between
you with gone ashore stories and fresh smart clothes.
Another coffee, another brandy which the Doctors
say don't drink, and you begin to feel the glow; the
glasses and cups mount and sparkle amongst little
white plates of prawns on the marble table before them
as they watch the lights around the harbour and the
occasional turning of tugs on the water.

'Don't forget us man,' he hears the silent distance of that
cold fucken Cape.

'That's why Liverpool is special son, we have a million
people who have seen such places. Our spirits walk
every stone of every port.' Johnny's eyes are shining
now with drink and love and God.

He's like Joey Besson who has just joined last trip on the deck and is not just a tyer of rope like you but a proper deckhand and more than once has pulled you up and knows more about the union and the past in a clearer way than you ever would. He comes from a big family but you burn with the reading, burn with the books, Joey always has a smile as though he's been there before you and left some time ago. A few times now you have a drink and end up gassing into the night; serious in the way you want to be but have too many things to think about to be worried long about terms and conditions and Joey casts his eye over you and says,

'What you're after is s good enough Jackie but it doesn't change anything for anyone else.'

And you cannot answer; the tight arse still within you for all the great causes. So you read deep into the night and sleep in the afternoon if you can get away with it; these are your days, the morning smoke and afternoon blow; cut out from the dark and the usual signals of drink and women; the constant search in the night and the looked for signs after you shake away the dust.

Clear now, showered and hair slicked down and clean shirt shining you duck out over the ropes and go sailing out, time and place and good fortune is all laid upon you and you forget the early mornings with the terrible wall at the back of the throat, croaking and kneeling with buckets to wash and damp down yesterday's dirt and scrape the rust off galley bars and decks. Staggering with plates that burn fingers and jugs that run and spill with milk and water, suffering, wilting in the first of the morning light, but later, later, always the reading to continue and time away from the ship, until after weeks of it, the blood runs up from the stomach and within his trousers there is a constant dripping wet.

'Slow down son, slow down,' Keogh says 'one hand for the company and one hand for yourself.'

The authority that is always there behind the freedom; you do the cleaning, the painting and the serving and even tie a rope now and then as you have the ticket even if it gives the deck crowd a laugh. Hardly a thought now to the orders that are posted there before the eyes each day. Take them in your stride Jackie you have another life now, the same as others have families; too many ideas swarming about inside you to be worried about any other fucker and you have to turn and catch yourself within the drift; who do you think you are, better than your Ma or Da ?

The unwritten law of this city, *never get above yourself.*
It is that that killed The Auntie.

Recovery: always a book stuffed in the back pocket
and finished with the drink; going home, a rest from
the coast and from the common search; a tired and
relaxed feeling with the shots of penicillin as they make
back to Liverpool on the warm tides of the Celtic Sea.

Mexico days: you are clear now of the needles and
the pain, can whistle in the blue air as even in this
part of the blitzed and bombed-out, blackened part
of this South end and there is a certain softness in the
paint and worn bricks in the evening sun. You walk
the sleepy streets to the dock and have a pint in the
Animal House with Nelly Flanagan who you've hardly
seen since the strike and she tells you they're going to
pull the whole square down and put up another corn-
flake box, the way they've ruined downtown and whole
districts of the North end and she shakes her head.

'They're pulling the guts out of everywhere. It makes
you sick son,' she says.

But Jackie knows she'll go on singing. She's that sort
of woman, as sad and cheerful as the wine lodge; som-
ersault time afterwards full of bucketed songs and

grimaces, crucified nights like the signs of any party by the river and you think of songs and laughter and the velvet and blue around you where shapes appear and disappear like ghosts and you meet in the wine madness of one Friday evening Alan Williams, cook off the *Diplomat*, who is out with his wife, dressed in his Sinatra suit with a waistcoat and a pork pie hat in the sticky heat of a Indian summer evening. Williams and his beautiful woman, equally well suited with a silk scarf and smear of lipstick across her pale half-Chinese face; a face that sees no mornings when he's home, only the grey early light before the sun and the taxi cutting its way through the quiet streets of Everton. Then the sleeping till noon and the going back to normal when he's away.

Jangling with them now through the singing weekend streets; groups of young girls with fellers draped around their necks, reel along in the pools of yellow light thrown down from the lamps and spill onto streets by the open doors of last order bars where you can peek inside and see the untouchables waiting in a huddle by the corner. Through the maze of offices and old warehouses people flood and stream through the streets to hit upon the clubs of blackened brick and insides bouncing with sounds like New York; wooden doors with iron bars across them and bouncers in tuxedos who want to look just like the movies, hair slicked down and rings on their fingers, gold teeth dancing when they laugh and your mind goes back five years when you used to cough da de da and tell them all you drink wine down on Tarleton Street.

'Fucken first tripper.'

Different clubs these, than the sweat-streamed walls of the crumbling cellar where you first learned to dance. You sit at a table with a drunken Barney Hayes in his clean Friday night shirt and tie askew and Williams, with his jacket off and waistcoat against the white cotton shirt who lights a long cigarette and beams over to the wife he calls 'girl.' And she, with a few wines inside her, hauls him up onto the floor and he shuffles around to the easy, slow music his porkpie hat hung on the corner of a chair.

Later, 'Don't want to go away either Jackie.' The unspoken fear, he looks at his wife, then cracks a smile. 'Give it a miss if I could,' a shake of the head and eyes looking down.

'Only exists for me to come home in a good suit, see her, pocket full of notes and a big Bronzie.' He nods at the water and the river.

'What would you do if you couldn't have that? Work in some factory somewhere? Skinning chickens, stirring ice cream, punching a clock, making sandwiches?'

He scrunches up his face and takes a drink at the thought of it. She doesn't say anything but holds her eyes fixed across the floor; Liverpool talk, in between worlds, nights full of dreams, The West Indies and Japan and Mexico and Tommy McCafferty's old man crying for his Islands as they sing and dance in Kirkby on New Year's Eve.

The Spain that is your Mexico, brown and silver as the river below; cities you dream about, the blue and black sea; the cold, gold-topped gassy beer with the ice drops glistening and falling on marble-topped tables awash with nuts and peeled shells and stubbed-out cigarettes in the saucers. Maybe our Auntie has dreamed it too in her grey post- war dream, her paradise when she visits Paris and Spain and Rome in her big bright black car and even meets the Pope; all too much for her when it is suddenly gone, when she sets fire to those dreams on the strength of all the spirits that walk these streets. Faraway cities on those mornings before the fire with nothing in them except the feel of winter; frost on the ground and dreams in the white rime that still clings to gable walls, corner attics, the

Malaga Jukebox, her lost song.

Book in hand and a wrapper of tobacco you lean back against the alleyway door in the sleepy, easy afternoons. Your Mexico in the blue light and haze of the Spanish coast all a glitter in the stillness. You look at the cover, book that first caught the eyes as you come aboard the *Barrister* and unknowing then the Horse about to drive you crazy through sweat and blood in the blasting sunlight of the Caribbean. *Lonesome Traveler* by Jack Kerouac, with its creased and crinkled pages and the front stained by drink; first found wedged between wooden bunk and mattress and quickly discarded on his first lonely ship; too much of his own loneliness then to worry about other demons. Now it's easy to think of that warm cabin, with the cold light that trickles in through the porthole as if by accident and settles on the bunk of a winters day cargo ship.

'*Lonesome Traveler*,' no thanks, too many things you had to do to survive but now it's the tales of traveler's you want but not by sea; but to work across America in cars and trains and Greyhound Buses and jump ships in between times and come back to cities that live on the ocean in your own time.

Our ship rides back from the Mediterranean like a prize-fighter, blown unscathed across Biscay and continues sweetly up the West coast to Glasgow. She discharges oranges and wine on the back of that big wind and is ready to sail to Liverpool again sooner than her scheduled time; the dream of every Chandler. Glasgow, a town like their own, a city full of dreams and madness; the banging, shouting shipyards; the lashed waters off the Clyde blown around every corner like shrapnel out of big Atlantic guns and Joey and himself and everyone else aboard drinking quickly in bars and clubs not to miss a sweet hour along Plantation quay.

Things get even better uptown when they are taken outside of themselves by others and the city sings and bounces like the edge of an upturned glass. Two women break away and dance with them in the Barrowlands, their faces turning into smiles as they take in the patter, smile and giggle, and allow their hands to be touched and be bought drink. Laughing women who sit on brown vellum cushions and on whose shoulders the night seems to sparkle to either stamps it with greatness or consigns it to the lot of the lonely.

The tall woman wears a velvet dress. Her hair is falling down. She kisses you and puts her tongue in your mouth as they dance. She comes downstairs to the yard out the back. Now, beside cardboard boxes and iron fire escapes, with leaves falling like feathers in the misty Autumn darkness, she helps you, fumbling with all her own kissing and arranging; leaning forward, her hands grip the edges of a dust bin like the goddess of a coaster bound for Sweden; her white legs incandescent as you pull up the fold skirt like a sail. Behind them are the crumbling damp bricks of the wall, ahead, the lozenges of alley light and music beating from the club.

Then the awkwardness and the terrible anxious sweating until she bends further and with great tenderness rests her arms lower and you hold her buttocks towards you.

Pushing again, head high in adventure, deeper as her hips roll their arcs under a wet moon; your dreams somewhere else as you rock away, her head down on the dustbin lid and her hands holding the handles like death. Inside your head, the moment another woman, that bastard Auntie overpowers you in an airless room and you grind out her name between your teeth, then the sound of her mouth open and crying; the smell of whisky and the sort of laughter that always comes with dancers. She's gone now.

'Jaysus, Oh Jaysus.'

This lovely woman's shoulders are bunched, her skirt as high as rigging on a mast. Different dreams adrift on the night as you fall into the sound of her cluttered gasps in this crumbling Glasgow yard. Her perfumed arms loosen on the bin handles. She miles and pats your head and arranges the dress closer to her and down over her knees. She would not be going home by bus.

When you get back Joey has his head on the table. His woman rolls her eyes like another sad souvenir for this city. She is making ready to go. Jackie's lover looks over and shrugs, the demands of friendship and company; it could have been a party: time adrift, from every corner bouncers mop up the evening's dregs.

'You can stick this place,' says Joey, gazing up.

The women say goodbye at the door. You walk with him falteringly in search of more drink and cross tumbling streets with dark alleys running off them with moonlight shining the slates. Car horns blare, their lights billow pink and yellow swathes cut across them. Cigarettes dangle and fall between their lips. They are away from forgotten ships.

'Some town this,' says Joey.

The neon down an alley says, 'Blues Club.' Red lights greet them and the night swims in and out again; all around them, night-time people; great flushes of energy in thick glasses, duffle coats black hair, corduroy caps, tartan scarves, a strange mix between them like the last burst of a shooting star, clearer at the point it fades than its passage across the sky. And the smells man; with coffee and wine and grass you've first tasted on the islands and outside, thoughts of cold blue skies of the French-Canadian winters instead of dank, misty Glasgow.

The realisation that you're finished with the sea comes not in a sudden flash but in a slow warm feeling that Junkies call a rush. It creeps around the bloodstream and envelopes you as if it had been waiting there all the time, just waiting for this moment like those old men on the tramps slinking from port to port year after year in sunshine and in rain until it no longer seems to matter what world they inhabit.

You tell Joey and he eyes you as though you've been a backslider all your life; ship to ship, company to company, port to port; another Paddy Bennett, another Johhny Keogh, as rebellious and as flaky as any casual, another O'Brien's cat. A dilettante.

'Here's you on about Communism and the strike. Ha ... fucken laugh that.'

They are told to shut up by a bouncer who looks like a Cunard Yank while another make believe Dylan twangs his guitar before them and the smoke hangs in a blue cloud around the stage. Joey puts his face up close.

'Communism is more than just a nice idea pal.'

He jerks his head in the direction of the singer. You roll a cigarette with great purpose and smooth the sweet tobacco down into the paper. The smell of the woman wraps the jangled nerves with the drug of high expectation and everything new.

'You're just escaping,' Joey says.

'You're just trying to get out.'

'You're a phony La, no one escapes.'

He looks away. 'You have to stand and fight wherever you are.'

The last of the stragglers leave the club with fresh

lipstick and little dabs of perfume in a flurry of banging taxi doors and you go back with Joey to the ship. You're finished; the decision as quick and slow as a lifetime passing, relentless and implacable before you. All the infinite possibilities slowly reined in one by one to this moment and then set free again on the autumn wind; the Atlantic night, the mighty Clyde, finished with it all. You're not a tight arse either but you want away, away from the rivers and docks and ships and constant jumping to the sound of bells.

Seventeen

You come up around the coast to Liverpool. 1968 Liverpool rocking in the Autumn night; how many stories are there to be told about this town? October, black and red; a decanted population about to be dispatched to hills and vales that surround the city and only back together in bright coloured buses for the match. The smoke across the sea of faces that roar at each other around the pitch; stanchions that rise out of this bulging heaving sea that curses and bellows and sways and roars and is transformed in the bathe of floodlights, the chips and pies, the smell of smoke; a shining cauldron as the air rises blue against the black night beyond the lights. Mexico dreams, a place of ships and rivers that he is leaving, The Auntie's song, the burning house.

'Remember Jackie, wherever you go, we all love you here.'

On Saturdays, the city at evening, the smell of the hamburger bars downtown. A painting in a cafe selling chips of a Palm boat from West Africa unloading cargo in the sun of the Queens docks, behind it the great brownstone Cathedral; trees, a blue sky over the

city and dockers and painters and platers and scrap-
ers, millions of them down the steps and stones of
history working their patterns into this town. Has it
changed you all this? All your hopes and fears against
the background of fire and the sea, a place of dancers
and shadows, of jokes and messages, an in between
world with the roll of a smoke, the sweep of sun over
the churches, the breaking of an egg, the crack of one
time into another. Can you see it now?

Some memory of what you are supposed to be, someone else outside as the ship comes up the river with
the weeping sky scratched red over Liverpool Bay and
you wash plates and scrub alleyways and haul rope
when called upon then are told to fucken go back
to your pantry as if your hands are no longer part of
you. Where is the glove-dusted magician, the quick-
silver glass, the broken jar, standing in line on winter
mornings, the shadows joining with the old family he
might have known?

What jangle as they approach the locks and voices
sing out on the far basin wall, the beckoners to this
black and dirty and beautiful city. The company is
well known. The shouting landing crew all part of
the crack that a short voyage brings, unlike the long
shadows when you are away months and everyone

looks on the return like an overture, the expectation all the greater like it must have been on the return of the tramps or whalers and all hell breaks loose for three days, where Tommy McCafferty's Da got marooned. The short trips carve their own likeness in faces on the rail, seamen looking; a city returning their gaze.

Liverpool air; the fire takes you away from Liverpool air, where the blood has run from many a pinched chest and ruined lung, and tosses you out into nights full of stars and canvas bivouacs hoisted above hatch-tops in glistening nights through the Caribbean. Now back to the same old smells, the tanneries, the molasses, the grain and sugar silos the falling rain spattering mud on the green warehouse doors and running black down the dockside cobbles; fire and songs bubbling up from your own city, but you have a wider family now not contained by isolated houses or salt sticking to the air.

The crowd below in the galley or on the deck littering every horizon from the Pacific to the Baltic sea; Catherine wheels exploding in the yellow dusk; all that's part of you. Liverpool, land of fantasy; the Western Approaches and the West Indies; Grenada, where Eddy stakes his vision from broken snatches of song and shaken heads. Where is he now with his hair sweeping down and his arms flung out? The

Saint who tells him after that last fight to look outside himself if he wants to be anyone; always the drink to warm the stories, Benny, the old fireman, Keogh the storekeeper, Barney Hayes the fighter; voices and memories seep away into the lilac evening. When you do break away, drunk outside the dockside parish, the alleyways and the stars, eyes close over and shoulders sag to the present as if tired of riding the nights, the books, the endless tales.

'Get outside of all this and you might learn something,' he says.

You open your eyes and see again the river. The green hills beyond give a relief to the docks and the warehouses and mills where the real city weeps and storms; between them with the shadows rising off the water you can see the six faces of the half-tide clock like a statue to the working class; the sun over the peninsula, the half white buildings beyond, the landing stage rising out of the water as great in its time as Chicago and New York; and let no one tell you the dockers do not know the great poem that is America; theirs is the experience of all the dynasties born on the waterside.

Before them, catering superintendents wait anxiously; half-tide lock gate-men with bicycle clips around their

trousers, customs officials, custom crews, deck superintendents, shore gangs, hangers' on, engine room,
'personnel,' shift watchmen four hours early, in line for
their big drink; all these shouting and trying to jump
aboard as the ship comes through the churning troughs
and great blackened wood of the inner gates and all
with a separate corner to protect and high above on a
bridge of burnished wood and polished brass the officers of the merchant marine with their usual disdain
tut tut at such lack of taste. It is the state of practice
in this queen of overtime ports; never a night when
there is not a docking gang to be raincoat-folded in
winter twilight nor the sweet smells of their tobacco
filling the top deck on the bus home.

You take it all in, this free theatre, the whole breadth of
an existence which unravels days and nights; the nod
of a head or the shape of a word, whole decades in the
making; the mock laughter amidst the shining glass,
the broken jar, the crowds on Lime Street or down the
landing stage; stood in line while the big ships take on
pantry assistants, saloon waiters, subterranean cleaners
and the chocolate favorites stand to one side like prize
cattle, smoothed hair and gold ringed against the grey
water; Cunard Yanks.

Stolen moments: in the ducking and weaving and

bringing home from broken crates or taking the ropes once in a while; there is more, much more and time has to be put aside to show others there is a wider picture, a bigger story but it's not just you . Who do you think you are, greater than your Ma and Da ? The docks are full of names and like the half tide clock cast within themselves and open to a wider world that both you and the city catch, a deck of cards, a kaleidoscope of long avenues, blue collar's; broad shoulders.

Coming alongside in the Queen's dock; the grip starts to loosen; the alleyways rage , a clump of boots, the bounce of shoulders off bulkheads, the poor dead Auntie and Uncle Billy and James Connolly, her lover just like Dockers and seamen, platers and wipers, screechers and gangers, crane men and tugboat men, catering crews and chandler's come marauding aboard; family Mafia's, street dynasties, company hucksters all singing their own song and you know it and don't know it, a sad happy place, a nation of cock eyed Celts..

The cabin is suddenly filled and you press drink into the welcoming hands; a home ship in her home dock. Break out another case and a carton of cigarettes, pass around the cans and catch the faces who suck in smoke and slurp at booze, laughing young faces, older ones, browner, more dignified; the lines in the ones of beaten brown watchman like his Dada, faces as lively as in a painting, the heirs of all your generation with their huge visions and great thirsts. Vera Cruz, Ah well!

Times are changing son, derelict shipyards across the river; the broken tenements and 'gardens' of the Inner City; Essex Street and Sussex Street and Warwick Street in the South end where the carters used to come with their dressed horses to wait on work. Changing son, going away in the flood that rolls back the second city of the once great Empire that has never considered itself England where the poor battle and batter each other for ships as they sleep in black rooms and pour down these streets to the docks along the river. Great Homer Street ablaze in the late afternoon; the sun striking yellow and a fiery red, and the old great houses bequeathed as slums for those that furnish the famine parishes. Great Howard Street, Great Mersey Street and Commercial Road all seething thoroughfares from where money has flown from many a bloodstained cargo to the river.

All this inside you; brimming with it, the crowd same as ever, unruffled or mad; a great chorus of babbling voices, the unfolding of the choirs within: another drink, the ale flows, the stories continue , one, then another until they run together, in rhythm, in perfect symmetry, the shine off the Tennant's tin, the Harp, the Guinness the sparkle of the consigned, the sweat starting to run: sweet tobacco and all the hope in the world.

Is it you then Jackie ,who sits there, tilting back in the chair and see faces staring back around the bunk, your voice shouting with theirs until the noise rings across the bulkheads, the brown table, the polished deck; fingers that turn and flush open more drink ; pour dark rum into little glasses and pass around cigarettes. Is this the dream you had in Poland? The voices sound no different, the lager is the same, the trips as lonely or full of laughs as light through a bottle, the smoke in the head. No time to worry where the cargo is transported from the yards, long or short voyages in the void; the shine of tarpaulins under the rain, pulled across groaning hatches full of cargo, where does it leave you to pick up a shilling; voices that are part of you but are gone; the gone man and across you generations flow like water.

How many seamen have come down and seen these dockside stations; black walls as if made of marble at some town in Ferrara, where the trains run on brown rusted lines built in another age. How many middays have they spent on the 'Pool with a quiet pint, the afternoon to hang around in, the night-times to kill; the sea a circle for all their days. The excitement of going away then the depressions on the tide; hope on the way home and in between, a world that only comes together in bits and pieces of broken moments. You ache to get away then get depressed in the river with the pier head disappearing behind you; Liverpool a place that is always somewhere else, but you are no more a hostage to its tides, nor the confines of its decks or the sunshine dancing on its bricks. Who are you kidding?

Drunk and weaving you say your goodbyes; strangely formal, they all laugh.

'Go on fuck-off.' Who d'you think you are? 'You'll be back next week.'

Laughing as well, no time for explanations; nothing to do with *the sea gets in your blood* bollocks that always bubbles up when anyone talks of getting out.

You walk ashore, mind awash, the wind on the water swinging the lights of the river as it curls downstream from the landing stage; free; never going back;1968 Liverpool October, red and black dreams dribbling into coming winter. How many stories are left to tell in this town, stories of arriving and leaving. December stories from New York, Spring stories from Barcelona Summer tales from Argentina; snow on the bridges of Osaka; the babble in his head, the babble in everyone's head who comes from around here.

There is a shout behind you and you look back over to the ship, luminous where she lies in the berth, a dark figure comes down from the foredeck where no light plays; a shadow you recognize as it comes closer. Joey has taken his bottle with the proper deck crew not these wannabe seafarers like you with papers stamped on the Scandinavian ticket; Joey still finishing the tying up when others are jangling below and you sit listening to voices. He emerges into the light and passes over the books he's borrowed from Bilbao. There's not much to say.

'Look after yourself Bud.'

'You too mate, I'll see you.'

All their dreams scattered on shipboard visions and now comes a silence in sombre October. Joey knows you're not kidding. You take the shiny covers and stow them and move on through the warehouses towards the Cunard buildings, the brighter lights, the bag held tight as if something might escape.

The voices are running together now, the few times that the shine is upon you; the extra strokes on the canvas, the gloss on a pint, the cool night air coming off the water, and even as you walk, the sweet thoughts of dreams and possibilities tumbling down; then a thud, the reverberations of the drink and a sudden smash of a brick through an abandoned warehouse. Kids run away at the sound of footsteps as you approach; the black row of desolation between dock wall and the dying heap mills, the chute overhead from the silo to the quay and the first container ships docking downriver.

You are sailing beneath high riding clouds, along dark waterside streets, the different shapes of gable walls and alleys in the shadows and higher outlines showing rows of chimney pots and television aerials tacked to crumbling stones like antennae towards the sky; bent conductors of a light that comes flickering and fragmented into every room and illuminates each figure in their own static dance. Shadowy visions visit you every evening and fly away at dawn. You want to be on their wings, on their tail, to arrive on the full flood and still be there when all else is quiet; to be stealing away on the mist, gone with the dawn.

You stop to roll a smoke and look; patches of light shine in pools where the twilight gangs continue. Along the road by the station, you buy matches at a kiosk run by a man whose legs are ruined by the docks and now sells newspapers silently busy in the red evening rush hour but now in the quiet time talks of times at sea.

'It's the only peace you'll get son. The peace of all the world.'

It doesn't matter you can say the same, the same as a million others from around here. You used to go away. Bucko Johnny, George Alexander, John Paul, you survived. No, you did more than survive, Liverpool the pearl in all our souls.